The

BINDING OF BOOKS

View of a Bookbinder's Workshop in 1689
— from an Engraving by Christopher Weigel

The
BINDING OF BOOKS

KENNETH F. PERRY • CLARENCE T. BAAB
Colorado State College
Greeley, Colorado

McKnight & McKnight Publishing Company
Bloomington, Illinois

Contents

6

Part III. Special Techniques and Problems

Introduction

Bookbinding as a craft is age old. Members of monastic orders laboriously produced hand lettered and illuminated sheets of parchment which were "bound" between boards covered with leather. It is interesting to note that even though we today have the most modern materials and equipment, the original basic binding processes remain the same.

As all crafts, bookbinding needs serious study and practice. Skill and knowledge are not acquired overnight. The first book bound will, like an initial effort in other areas, reflect the need for continued experiences. The work will be interesting, but it will not necessarily be easy. It will be a kind of work with many challenges, and the opportunities for original thinking are great. With the acquisition of skill and knowledge, a binder can become an artist in the true meaning of that term.

The binding of books can be adapted to the limitations of any kind of workshop from a table in the corner of a room to the most modern workshop. Both the amateur and expert will find possibilities within the field to meet almost any interest or ability. This work may vary from simple pamphlets to full leather bindings and may extend into inlay work, hand tooling, and ornamentation with gold leaf, not to mention marbling and gilt edging. Limitless opportunities are afforded for pleasing effects with color and the interesting use of leather, coated fabric, impregnated fabric, book cloth, and paper.

9

The craftsman who is not satisfied with binding books can study the wide fields of leather and paper manufacture; design, upon which so much of the final effect of his work depends; the history and romance of the craft; ancient manuscripts now housed in famous museums; and the art of illumination. Each individual, too, will find work suited to his ability and can experiment with simple or elaborate bindings, as his taste or interest directs. Magazines, newspapers, blank pages bound together for cookbooks or scrapbooks, sheet music or music books bound for convenience of use or to preserve the life of the material, reconditioning valuable books, or the binding of manuscripts into book form—all offer challenges to the craftsman.

Avocational as well as the vocational interests of man may be met through the binding of books. Bookbinding includes repair work, rebinding old volumes, or the complete binding of new books. Repairing varies from the placing of a piece of transparent gummed tape over a torn page to the complete rebinding of a volume.

Variations from the binding of books, which can be done with the same materials and equipment and which will appeal to the craftsman, include novelty book covers, notebook covers, covers for phone books, bridge score pads, and many other articles for use about the home, office, church, school, or library.

The necessary tools, equipment, materials, and supplies are each treated in subsequent chapters. After a discussion of the problems of binding, step-by-step procedures for the binding of full-, half-, and quarter-bound books are presented. These processes have been used for many years in high school and college binding classes and have proved to be valuable guides to the beginner. To the advanced student of binding they serve as reference material to assist in special problems.

Part I

General Information

Chapter 1

The Parts of a Book

Books today are everywhere. No matter where we are, we see them — at the newsstand of the depot or airport waiting room, on the doctor's reference shelf, the lawyer's office, the school classroom, and in the telephone booth. To some individuals, books supply needed information. To others, they provide hours of entertainment. They bring us the reports of the most recent research, and at the same time, books are storehouses of the records of antiquity.

Books come in all sizes with all types of binding. Some are paperbound and inexpensive. Others are bound in rich leather. The pages or sections of some are held together with an adhesive or a staple, while others, such as music books, dictionaries, and Bibles, are sewed so they will remain open when in use.

The history of man has been recorded in paintings, on cave walls, in chiseled inscriptions on stone, on papyrus, and on the parchment of the monastic orders. But today's storyteller or historian has the advantage of modern design with type, durable bindings, and papers to fit every purpose.

The Elements of a Book

Books come in a wide variety of sizes, shapes, colors, and qualities. These will range from the simple paper-covered memo pad to the beautiful leather-bound volume, the product of the artist craftsman. Each will have at least two things in common: (1) sheets or leaves make up the body, and (2) a cover protects and/or decorates the volume.

The simple memo book, when examined closely, will be seen to be made up of individual sheets held together, along with the cover, by one or two staples. Books, originally, followed this simple plan — single sheets fastened together at the back in one manner or another.

When a modern textbook or novel is looked at from the top or bottom, one may see along the binding edge several groupings of folded leaves. These units are called signatures and may consist of 8, 12, 16, 24, 32, 48, 64, or more pages.

Holding the Body Together

The body of a book, its combined signatures, must be fastened together to form a single unit. This may be done in a variety of ways.

Sewing

The most common method of holding together the body of a hardbound textbook or novel is *sewing*. Any one of a number of methods may be employed which may be classed as follows:

1. *Center sewing* — sewing through the center of each signature and chaining these stitches together (loom or Smythe sewing).

2. *Side sewing* — sewing vertically through the body of the book from front to back.

3. *A combination* (in hand binding) of center and side.

Mechanical Fasteners

Paper-covered books are often held together with metal or plastic fasteners. Staples, nails, coils of wire, and formed plastic strips are commonly used. Stapling, as sewing, may be *center* or *side* and is often called *wire stitching*. A form of stapling used for large scrapbooks, wallpaper sample books, and similar binding problems is *nailing*. The use of wire coils and plastic strips is often called *mechanical binding*.

Fastening with Glue

One of the more recent methods of holding the body of a book as a unit employs glue and is called *perfect binding*. Familiar examples are the popular paperbound books available in drugstores, hotels, supermarkets, and air terminals. In *perfect binding*, the individual leaves are fastened together with a flexible glue, which also holds the cover in place.

Methods of Sewing

In hand binding any one of several methods of sewing is employed. The use of the book will usually be the determining factor in choosing the sewing method to be used.

Flat stitching is a *side sewing* method. The hand binder is usually restricted to relatively thin books when using this method; that is, volumes which will be 3/4″ thick or less. Holes must be made in the body for the stitches which cross on the back of the book.

Machine stitching is another side sewing method. Holes are drilled or punched and the book is sewed twice, up and down through the holes.

Overcast sewing is a combination of flat stitching and chain sewing. The hand binder uses this method when a thick book must be handled. Signatures are sequentially side sewed, one to another.

Loom sewing is a form of center or edge sewing used when the finished book must stay flat when opened. It is not as strong as the side sewing methods but can be made very serviceable.

Saddle sewing is restricted to books having, in effect, a single signature. This method of sewing is similar to machine stitching, with the difference being that the work is done in the center of the opened fold, rather than through the side of the body.

The Cover

As with the body of the book, the finished cloth cover is composed of a number of individual pieces. The covering material is usually a form of cloth although sheet plastic, leather, paper, and other sheet products may be used. For memo pads or inexpensive books and pamphlets, a heavy paper or plastic sheet will often comprise the total cover.

Boards of specially constituted paper are usually used for the stiffener material in the cover. Again, almost any heavy cardboard can be utilized, but the *hard-rolled binder's board* is commonly used. The main requirement is a relatively thin, stiff material, which can be cut and formed easily and cleanly and which will flex under heavy pressure.

Inside the cover material at the *backbone* or *spine* of the book is a piece of heavy paper — *the back lining*. The cover materials are assembled with the proper spacing and fastened together with glue.

Fastening the Body to the Cover

Although the preparation of the cover and assembly of the body of the volume require the major portion of the time and material used in binding a book, it is the manner of fastening them together that most frequently determines the life of the binding.

Endsheets and Backing Material

If a commercially bound book is examined closely, a heavy paper endsheet will be noted in the front and at the back. Half of this folded sheet is glued to the cover; the other half is glued to the side of the body along a narrow strip at the back.

Beneath this endsheet, at the joint of cover and body, a slight ridge will be seen. This ridge is formed by a reinforcing material which has been glued to the back of the body and caught in the gluing of the endsheet to the cover. *Backing flannel* or *super cloth* is used for this purpose.

In the binding described, a typical mass-produced book, the cover and body are held together by the gluing of the super to the body and to the board. The degree to which the book will stand hard use depends upon the quality of the glue and super material used.

Other Reinforcements

To give a greater quality to the binding, a variety of reinforcing methods may be used.

Jointed Endsheets

Instead of a single, folded-paper endsheet, two pieces of endsheet paper may be joined with a strip of muslin which is sewed along with the body of the book. As a result, the strain is applied to the cloth attached to the body, rather than to a narrow strip of reinforcing material, or to the narrow glue attachment of the endsheet to the body.

Reinforcing End Signatures

If the book is chain sewed through the back of the signatures, narrow muslin strips may be glued to the end signatures, which in turn are glued or "tipped." The muslin strip will stand more flexing of the thread and a stronger pull than would paper alone.

More Than One Super

To make possible the rapid handling of mass-produced books, commercial binders must use quick-setting glues and supers of cheesecloth, while for the same purpose, the hand binder uses a *backing flannel*. Often two supers are applied to the back of the body. Each is glued separately and one often extends a greater distance onto the cover board.

Other Parts of a Binding

Narrow decorative strips, called *headbands,* are often used at the top and bottom of the spine to cover the edge of the glued back. They do not extend onto the cover and do not add strength to the binding. Headbands are a purely decorative finishing touch to the binding.

Chapter 2

General Types of Bindings

Specifications for commercial binding include information about the type of sewing, reinforcements, weight of end-sheet material, thickness of board, and quality of cover material. Within each of these, there are various levels of quality and cost.

As the hand binder determines the type of binding to be done, he must also make judgments on these factors.

Classification of Bindings

The binder will frequently make a basic description of a binding by its type of cover or type of sewing. Commercially, two higher quality bindings would include *library binding* and *textbook binding*.

Types of Covers

Covers generally fall into four types described as:
1. Full bound
2. Quarter bound
3. Half bound
4. Three-quarter bound

Each of these is fully described later in this book.

18

Types of Sewing

Several types of hand sewing have already been listed. There are five groups as follows:
1. Flat Stitching
2. Machine Stitching
3. Overcast Sewing
4. Loom Sewing
5. Saddle Sewing

In Part Two of this book, detailed instructions are given as to how these types of sewing may be done by the hand bookbinder.

In commercial binding, though, machines are used to fasten the body together. In *Smythe sewing,* the signatures are stitched through the center fold, with each signature knotted to the preceding one. A Smythe-sewed book opens flat, and the thread may be seen in the center of each signature.

Side-sewed and *saddle-sewed books* are described as *McCain* or *Singer* sewed. As in the machine stitch of the hand binder, each book is sewed through from front to back as a single unit. This method of sewing is very strong, but the book must be held open by the reader.

Edition Binding

The typical binding of a novel, as described in Chapter 1, is satisfactory for its use in the personal library by the purchaser. As was mentioned earlier, an *edition* binding of any type is only as strong as the glued fastening of supers and endsheets.

Library Binding

Books which are to be placed on the shelves of libraries will receive much harder wear than those in personal libraries. Library-bound books and textbooks have heavier board, better quality covering materials, and are frequently reinforced with jointed endsheets. If Smythe sewed, reinforcements are added to the first and last signatures.

Special Types of Bindings

The hand binder is frequently called upon to bind magazines, newspapers, and other large or unusual materials. He must be familiar with the use to which each book is to be put and must make proper allowance for durability as he determines the type of sewing and the quality of cover material. Bibles, music books and other volumes which must lie flat when in use will need to be loom-sewed. The cover treatment for even such a simple volume as a single-fold pamphlet can be made interesting.

Types of Covers

Bindings can be classified according to the type of cover used. These covers ordinarily include four types:

Quarter-Bound Books

In quarter-bound books, the back is traditionally made from leather, and the sides are selected from pyroxylin-treated fabrics, vinyl, or starch-filled book cloth. The back material of quarter-bound books extends over the side one-eighth the width of the side as shown in Figure 1.

Many books are quarter bound in combinations other than leather and coated fabric, a common one being coated fabric or book-cloth back with paper sides. Other combinations of materials are also to be found.

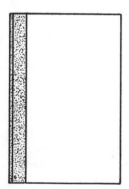

Fig. 1. Quarter-Bound Book

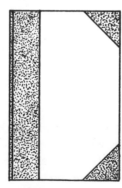

Fig. 2. Half-Bound Book

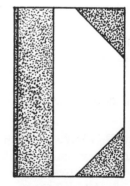

Fig. 3. Three-Quarter-Bound Book

Half-Bound Books

Half-bound books differ from three-quarter-bound books only in the distance which the back material extends over the front and back covers. On half-bound books this back material extends over the covers one-fourth the width of each cover. The corners on a half-bound book are smaller than those on three-quarter-bound books because they are only one-fourth the width of the cover. See Figure 2. Methods for determining size of corners are described in the instruction processes. Half-bound books are "sided up" with suitable binding materials.

Three-Quarter-Bound Books

Books which have the back and four corners made from the same material (usually leather), and which are "sided up" with coated or impregnated fabrics, book cloth, or other material, are either half- or three-quarter bindings. On books where the back material extends over the side one third the width of the cover, the book is a *three quarter binding*. It is this "one-third-the-width-of-the-cover" distance which determines that it is a three-quarter binding. See Figure 3. In the true three-quarter binding, the width of the corner is measured to equal one-third the width of the side. Three-quarter bindings may be sided up with pyroxylin-treated fabrics, book cloth, buckram, or sometimes paper.

Full-Bound Books

Those books whose covers are made entirely from one kind of binding material such as leather, coated fabrics, buckram, canvas, gingham, book cloth, vinyl, vellum, or oilcloth are called *full-bound books*. It is also possible to make a cover of paper, though it would be impractical in most cases. In full-bound books, only one piece of binding material is used, and when more than one piece is used it ceases to be a full-bound book. Four full-bound books, each covered with a different binding material, are shown in Figure 4. From left to right the books are bound in coated fabric, oilcloth, leather, and linen.

Standard Binding Fabrics

Coated Fabrics

Materials which have a woven back and a heavy coating of pyroxylin or other cellulose compound are referred to in this book as *coated fabrics*. These materials come with many different grains and patterns. Occasionally, they are referred to as imitation leather. They appear under many trade names, such as Fabrikoid, Keratol, Sturdite, Lacqroid, and Terek.

Coated fabrics differ from impregnated fabrics in the great amount of surface coating. Here most of the patterns or grains appear in the coating itself, rather than in the original cloth base.

For but little additional expense, coated fabrics may be purchased with a special finish which does not require a size for lettering; it also saves an application of adhesive coating since glue will stick to it.

Impregnated Fabrics

Book cloths, buckrams, and certain natural cloths which have been saturated in a pyroxylin solution and allowed to dry are called *impregnated fabrics*. Sometimes the back side of these materials is sized to insure the glue sticking to the fabric.

Fig. 4. Four Full-Bound Books

Impregnated fabrics differ from coated fabrics in the amount of surface coating. When a grain or pattern is applied to impregnated fabrics, it is worked directly into the cloth of buckram rather than on a surface coating as in the case of the coated fabrics.

Starch-Filled Fabrics

Book cloths or buckrams which are not treated with pyroxylin are commonly starch filled to give the material "body." Such material is not waterproof, and care must be taken to keep it clean when working with it.

Ordinarily, these fabrics have the same base as the material which is used in making impregnated fabrics.

Vinyl

During the last decade, the new material which has offered the greatest advance in cover making is the non-woven vinyl plastic cover stock. This material is now available from the same sources which provide pyroxylin-coated fabrics. Vinyl fiber or unsupported vinyl plastic is also available in several weights and qualities for electronic heat sealing which is done commercially by several loose-leaf binding concerns. All vinyls are waterproof and are available in weights and colors for all uses. Typical of several trade names for this material would be Veroseal Virgin Vinyl.

Typical Bindings of Books

Fiction books, schoolbooks, hymnals, and other books in common use should be bound in full-coated fabrics or in impregnated buckram. These materials are waterproof and may easily be cleaned. While their cost is more than ordinary book cloth or cheaper materials, they are recommended because they can be cleaned easily and are very durable.

Where expense is an item, cheaper materials may be substituted. However, if the book is to have considerable use, *the best material will usually prove to be the cheapest.*

The Binding of a Magazine

The binder of magazines is confronted with several problems not common to the binding of other kinds of books. In the first place, magazines are usually printed on heavy coated paper, thus making the finished volume heavier than the average book. This, together with the fact that they are usually larger than most books, requires stronger binding methods and the use of heavier materials. Magazines should be bound for permanence because it is impossible to obtain back numbers after a few years. The binder should carefully determine the best method of sewing and should select a heavier grade of binding material than used on ordinary books. The strongest binding materials should be used at the points of greatest wear, which are the joints, corners, and the bottom of the cover boards. For this reason the half- or three-quarter leather binding is recommended. Heavy weight impregnated buckram is also satisfactory if full binding is desired. Magazines are usually bound with this material. Coated fabrics may crack.

Binding Music Books

Music books are required to lie flat on a stand or rack, and for this reason some type of loom sewing (see page 97) should be used to permit the pages to remain open at any place. The type of binding on a music book is not as important as the type of sewing. While loom sewing is not as strong as other methods, the pages remain open and flat while in use and this is perhaps the most important item for consideration. Obvious exceptions to this method would be individual copies of sheet music or manuscripts in single pages.

The kind of material required will depend upon the use the volume will receive.

Binding Newspapers

Volumes of newspapers should be bound in a heavy buckram or canvas because of their size. If full bindings are too expensive, half bindings using buckram or canvas corners and backs sided up with paper or some other cheaper binding material may be used. If care is used in putting on the corners and back strip, some expense may be saved by not siding up the covers but leaving the cover board exposed.

Newspapers are usually sewed by the overcast method, or they may be nailed if the volume is a thick one. If the volume is thin (not more than one inch in thickness) often it may be machine stitched (see page 95).

Nailing is mentioned here because it is occasionally used, but it is not generally recommended. However, if a page has a wide inside margin and economy and speed are factors, the method can be employed, though quality is obviously sacrificed. Nailing and fastening by wire are expeditious methods only, but may find some use, as for binding a professor's thick syllabus that will be used for only one or two semesters and will be thrown away when his book is published.

Binding Single-Fold Pamphlets

A single-fold pamphlet may be bound with any kind of material, but since it is desirable to allow the pages to lie flat, the method of sewing is more important than the type of binding. It is suggested that such pamphlets be sewed with the saddle stitch (see page 101) and the choice of binding be made in terms of the use to which the volume is to be put.

Binding Bibles

Bibles may be bound in any type of binding, although the full-leather overlapping and/or semi-overlapping method is usually used, in which a levant-grain morocco goat leather or substitute is employed. The edges of the leather extend beyond the solid part of the cover so that they can be "formed" over the book, which makes the "deluxe" type of binding, Figure 5. In Bibles, as in music books, the type of sewing used is more important than the type of binding. The margins are usually very narrow on the back edges of the pages, which makes some type of loom sewing necessary. Another reason for using this method of sewing is that when the Bible is opened its pages

Fig. 5. Deluxe-Bound Bible

are allowed to lie flat. Work on a Bible should be undertaken only after a craftsman has developed considerable skill. It is not a project for the beginner.

Determining the Type of Binding

The type of binding to be used on a book depends upon three things: (1) the size of the book; (2) the use of the book; and (3) the restrictions on the cost of materials to be used. These three criteria are used in the following example:

A man's hobby is the collecting of Scotch jokes which he mounts in a book to be used only occasionally. Here Scotch-plaid gingham may be used to advantage. It will be seen that under these conditions a cloth binding is adequate and suitable for the purpose. If, however, this book were to be handled by many readers it would soon become soiled and could be cleaned only with great difficulty.

The above example points out the desirability of using coated fabrics, vinyl, or impregnated buckram if many individuals are to use the book. This would include most school, library, and church books.

As has already been indicated, magazines should be put in the best type of binding possible in terms of the money available. A half or three-quarter leather binding is always to be recommended. However because of cost, heavy buckram is probably the most practical. Large books—newspapers and the like—should be bound in heavy binding materials with the strongest methods possible.

Determining the Repair Needed by a Book

The smallest repair to keep a book in condition for use is perhaps the placing of transparent gummed tape over torn pages. All torn places should be repaired at once, and every effort made to secure a tape that will not discolor. This simple repair is appropriate for such volumes as textbooks and hymnals that will be discarded when well worn. Torn pages of library books and personal volumes should be mended with strips of fibrous Japanese tissue paper and paste. Never should a binder attempt even a simple repair on a valuable book until he has acquired skill and possesses a knowledge of correct procedures.

If a book is generally in good condition but has one or two loose pages, they may be glued or tipped (not to exceed ⅛ inch) and replaced. However, if there are several loose pages, the book should be removed from the cover and rebound.

Many times books tear loose from the covers at the joint. In this case new endsheets are applied and, with a few other operations described in the chapter on repair, the book is returned to the original cover.

When a cover becomes badly worn or broken, though the book itself is in good condition (no loose pages and the sewing still tight), new endsheets are generally applied to the book and the book is bound in a new cover.

We have all seen the book with a "broken back"—i.e., the place where the glue and super cloth or reinforcement material break between sections. This book always opens at this place and occasionally is held only by a few threads. In correcting this break it is recommended that the book be torn down, resewed, and replaced in the old cover if it is still good. Such repairs as the use of gummed or adhesive tape, or tipping with glue or paste are not satisfactory and may prove costly.

However, if the sewing is still good, the book should be removed from the cover and the reinforcing material removed. New endsheets should be cut and applied and new reinforcement material glued onto the back.

Book collectors or expert binders of valuable books should always be consulted before attempting to make any kind of a repair on volumes having monetary or sentimental value. Old books, especially, should not be touched in any way until after competent advice is received. Oftentimes the value of a book is seriously decreased because the binder has not sought such advice.

Weakened sewing occasionally permits the loosening of sections, and while the pages and back are all in good condition the book becomes "loose." The breaking of a single thread will sometimes bring this about and the only remedy is a complete resewing.

Determining the Proper Type of Sewing

The condition of the sewing on a book can generally be determined by locating the center of any section, and snapping the threads with the fingernail to see if the sewing has "life." If it is in good condition, the threads will snap back into place; if broken, they will remain out. This test should be made several places in the book. If the sewing is good, the book need not be resewed; if loose or broken, the entire book must be torn down and resewed.

On schoolbooks or volumes used by many individuals, the overcast method of sewing should be employed if the book is more than $1\frac{1}{2}''$ in thickness. If it is less than $1\frac{1}{2}''$ thick, it should be machine stitched. Books not exceeding $\frac{3}{4}''$ in thickness may be flat stitched, though the machine stitch is preferable.

Music books, Bibles, or other volumes which are to lie flat when open should be loom sewed. If there are many loose pages, the thickness of the book will determine the method of sewing as indicated above.

Single-section pamphlets, if the pages are not loose, should always be sewed with the saddle stitch, which allows the page to lie flat when opened. If the pamphlet has loose sheets, it should be flat stitched or machine stitched.

Chapter 3

Tools and Equipment

At one time all binding was done by hand with relatively simple equipment. While little change has been made in the requirements of hand methods, the tools have undergone improvement. However, the greatest improvement has been made in the machines now used by large bookbinding companies. These are described in Chapter 5.

Most of the tools necessary for hand binding are inexpensive and can easily be made or purchased. If the student or home craftsman has a knack of adapting materials to his need, he can convert many ordinary tools into usable hand equipment and may with little difficulty outfit a small bindery.

Minimum Tools and Equipment

The following tools or suitable substitutes are necessary for hand binding:

Shears (8 inch preferred—Figure 6)
Scratch awl (Figure 7)

Fig. 6. Shears

Fig. 7. Scratch Awl

Rule or good yardstick
Bone folder (can also be made from hard maple —
    Figure 8)
Cobbler's hammer (Figure 9)
Backsaw (14 to 16 point—Figure 10)
Needles—No. 1/0 harness needles
Cutting knife (common paring knife or good pocket knife)
Straightedge (steel—36 inch)
Pencil (hard)
Skiving knife (for leather—Figure 11)
Hand drill
$\frac{3}{32}$" drill bits

Many of the above items are to be found about the home or school and are all that are necessary for simple binding.

The *shears* are used to cut endsheets, joint strips, flannel, and other materials; the *awl* for punching the book for sewing or turning round corners. If the book is to be sewed on the loom, the *saw* is used for "sawing-in." The *straightedge* and *knife* are used to cut the boards for covers—a heavy pocketknife being better for this purpose than the paring knife. The *bone folder* is used to fold the endsheets, to make up the cover, and to turn the edges of the cover. It may also be made of maple, but should be waterproofed. The *cobbler's hammer* is used for pounding off old glue, rounding, backing, and other hammering purposes.

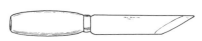

Fig. 8. Bone Folder

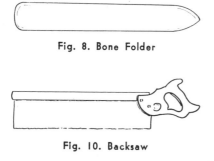

Fig. 10. Backsaw

Fig. 11. Skiving Knife

Fig. 9. Cobbler's Hammer

Additional Helpful Tools and Equipment

Additions to this list which will be found most useful but which are not absolutely required are *dividers*, Figure 12; *pliers*, Figure 13; an *oyster knife*, Figure 14; and a *backing hammer*, Figure 15. The dividers are used on one-half and three-quarter bindings for spacing out the lettering strip and laying off corners for the siding-up material. The pliers and oyster knife (or staple extractor) are useful in removing staples from old books and magazines. A backing hammer is most satisfactory, especially in a school or commercial shop. All work except trimming, rounding, and backing can be done with these simple tools. However, to complete a small home or school bindery the following equipment is necessary (detailed information for its construction will be found in the latter part of the chapter):

A *finishers' clamp* is used to hold the book for the "sawing-in" operation, hand lettering, and rolling gold lines. (See Figure 26.)

A **V** *trough* is needed for punching saddle-stitched books. (See Figure 27.)

A *sewing frame* is used to hold the book while it is being "loom sewed," Figure 16.

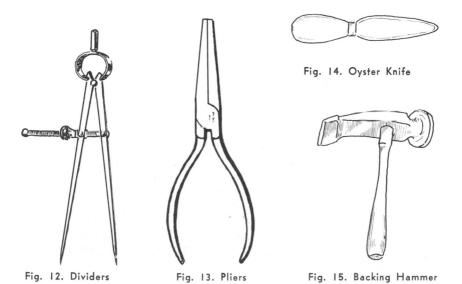

Fig. 14. Oyster Knife

Fig. 12. Dividers   Fig. 13. Pliers   Fig. 15. Backing Hammer

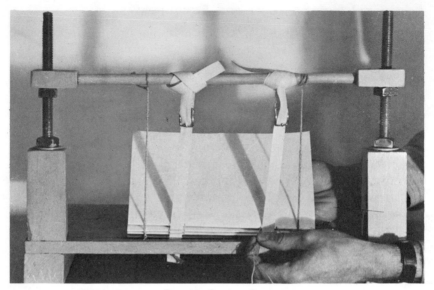

Fig. 16. Sewing Frame

Fig. 17. Punching Guide

Fig. 18. Stabbing Machine

If a book is to be sewed by either the overcast, machine-stitch, or a flat stitching method, the book needs to be punched by using a *punching guide,* Figure 17, or a *stabbing machine,* Figure 18. A punching guide may also be made from a piece of binders board, as will be shown later. (See Figure 30.)

One step in the binding process requires that the *edges of the book be trimmed or smoothed.* This operation may be carried out in one of four ways, and for this purpose one or more of the following tools or equipment may be purchased or constructed:

1. The best method is to obtain a small *cutting machine,* Figure 19, though this is expensive.

2. A most satisfactory result is obtained with a *belt or disk sander,* Figure 20. Care must be taken to keep the book square.

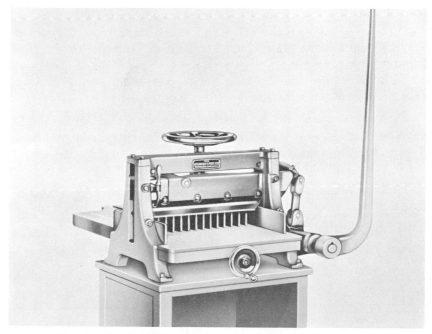

Fig. 19. Small Cutting Machine (Courtesy Chandler & Price)

3. A *plough-and-cutting press* was used as one of the first methods for accomplishing this step although it is most difficult for beginners to use.

4. A *beveled chisel* on a special finisher's clamp may be used, Figures 21 and 32.

5. If no equipment is available, it is possible to *sand the book by hand* when it is held in the finishers' press previously mentioned.

A *pounding iron*, sometimes called an *iron beating block*, is necessary for rounding books and hammering off old glue. If a smooth piece of iron is not available, a heavy piece of hard maple or birch may be used. A piece of iron ½ an inch thick may be procured on special order from a metal supply house. Your local junk yard may have such an item. Be sure one surface is smooth.

Another step in binding is to *back the book*. One of three pieces of equipment may be used for this purpose:

1. A *backer*, obtainable from a bindery supply company, is perhaps the best, though the most expensive, Figure 22.

2. A *combination backer and press* made from hardwood, four carriage bolts and some strap iron, can be used. (See Figure 33.)

3. *Backing boards*, held between a hand screw or in a vise, work rather effectively. (See Figure 34.)

A *letterpress* can be used to press books after endsheets have been glued and for all other jobs requiring even pressure, Figure 23. The combination backer and press mentioned above

Fig. 20. Sanding a Book
with a Disk Sander

Fig. 21. Trimming with a
Beveled Chisel — Book Held
in the Finisher's Clamp

may be used for this purpose, though when many books are being bound the letterpress is desirable. If one or two steel bench screws are available, a larger press and backer may easily be constructed at the end of a strong workbench.

Pressing tins are required to press in the joints of a book and to allow the endsheets to dry flat. When the combination backer and press is used, only flat tins are necessary. When the letterpress is used, two sets are required—flat ones between endsheets and additional tins with the edge turned over to press in the joint. The latter are made from 14 or 16 gauge rustproof metal.

A *double boiler* or a gas or electric *gluepot* will be helpful, Figure 24.

A *work table* or bench is often a good investment.

A *vise* will prove handy though it is unnecessary if the combination backer and press is built to permit both backing and pressing.

Lettering may be done with an *electric pen*, Figure 25, which transfers gold or foil to the book. As this is initially tried, it may produce a "homemade" result, but the skillful and

Fig. 22. Backer   Fig. 23. Letterpress

Fig. 24. Electric Gluepot

Fig. 25. Lettering a Book
with an Electric Pen

imaginative individual can produce professional effects. *Gold lettering machines* do the best work if the craftsman goes into binding seriously enough to afford one. Simpler forms of this operation are performed with white or colored ink applied with an ordinary writing pen.

When the situation demands higher production output, a *casemaking gauge* should be obtained or made.

When *gold lines* are desired on the backs of books, one of two methods may be used in applying them. If the workman has a *lettering machine,* different lengths of brass rule should be used to apply these lines. However, if a lettering machine is not available, *hand rolls* may be obtained or made.

A *hand pallet* is used for gold lettering by hand.

If lines are desired on the back of the books and rolls are to be used instead of brass rule in the lettering machine, a *roll gold cushion* is needed so as to make the gold accessible at all times with a minimum amount of waste.

Constructing the Necessary Equipment

Almost any piece of equipment thus far described can be constructed by anyone handy with tools, or may be built by a cabinetmaker and a machinist at a reasonable cost.

The *finishers' clamp* is constructed of two 1″ x 4″ pieces of hardwood and two ⅜″ x 4″ carriage bolts. Although the length may vary, 14″ is sufficient for average binding purposes, Figure 26.

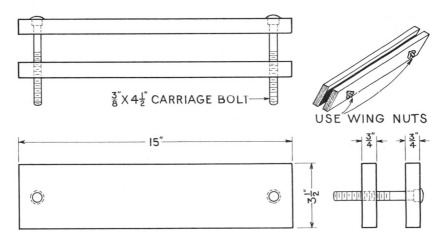

Fig. 26. Finisher's Clamp

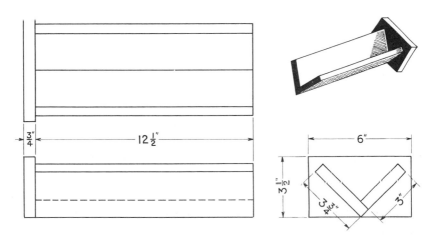

Fig. 27. V Trough

A **V** *trough* may be made from ends of boxes or scraps of wood which may be found around the home or school shop, Figure 27.

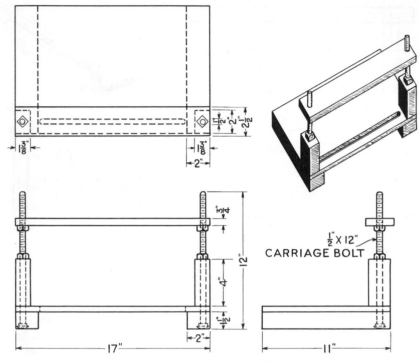

CARRIAGE BOLT
$\frac{1}{2}$" X 12"

Fig. 28. Adjustable Sewing Frame

The best *sewing frame* is adjustable because tapes and cords can be regulated easily, Figure 28. A simpler frame, using thumbtacks to tighten the cords or tapes, may be used, Figure 29.

One method of making a *punching guide* is to use a piece of binders board to space off the holes to be punched with a scratch awl, Figure 30.

Another method is to use scraps of board and an adjustable gauge so the awl or series of awls will be evenly spaced, Figure 31.

A *stabbing machine* is by far the best to use for this purpose because of its sturdiness and long life. Its high cost is the only disadvantage.

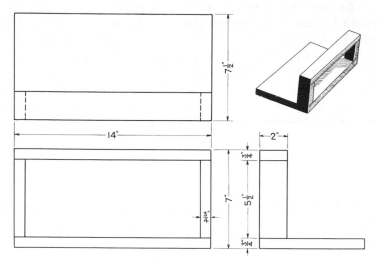

Fig. 29. Sewing Frame (Box)

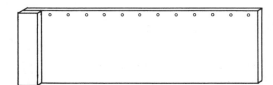

Fig. 30. Punching Guide made of Binders Board

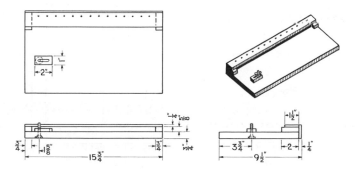

Fig. 31. Adjustable Punching Guide

To use the *beveled chisel,* one piece of wood 2 inches thick and exactly the same size as one side of the finishers' clamp, Figure 26, is needed to "steady" the chisel in cutting. (See Figure 21.) The chisel is made from a regular one-inch woodworking chisel. It is ground off and sharpened at an angle of thirty degrees, Figure 32. The cutting is generally done with the point, although successful cutting can be done with the "heel." *Keep this tool sharp.*

Fig. 32. Beveled Chisel

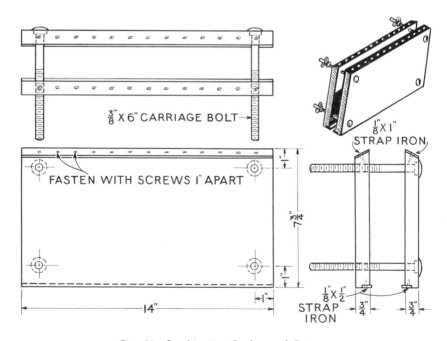

Fig. 33. Combination Backer and Press

A *combination backer and press* may be constructed from hardwood or ¾ inch plywood as shown in Figure 33. Holes should be bored and dowels inserted for strength if wood other than plywood is used.

The *pounding iron* may be secured at almost any junkyard, being only a thick piece of metal, smooth on one side. It

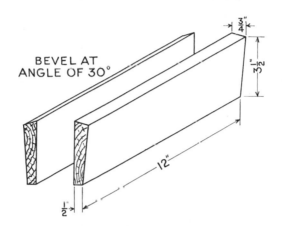

BEVEL AT
ANGLE OF 30°

Fig. 34. Backing Boards

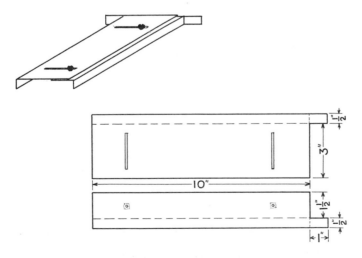

Fig. 35. Adjustable Casemaking Gauge

can be of any size larger than the books to be bound. A thick piece of hardwood may be substituted if necessary.

Backing boards will produce more satisfactory results when they are made from hardwood, Figure 34.

Two types of *casemaking gauge* are shown here: (1) An adjustable one, Figure 35, which is most desirable; and (2) one which is not adjustable, Figure 36. A piece of wood planed to the width of the needed space, less the thickness of two pieces of metal, may also be used for a gauge, Figure 37.

Common sizes of *pressing tins* are 6½" x 9½" and 9½" x 12½". The smaller size may be used with all fiction books, the larger size with all other books. Four tins are usually required for each book, although flat tins alone are necessary when the combination backer and press is used. The two flat tins are made of 24-gauge galvanized iron, and those with the edge turned (about 3/32") of 16-gauge. These may be obtained from any tin shop.

It is best to have *rolls* made from brass to the dimensions as shown in Figure 38. It is perhaps cheaper to buy used rolls if the workman does not have a metal lathe and forge, or must have them made to order.

Various lengths of *brass rule* may be used to put lines on the backs of books by using a lettering machine. The amateur will find this method the most satisfactory. (See pp. 129 and 143.)

A *roll-gold cushion* may be made from wood and a small piece of leather, Figure 39. If a brass rule is used in the lettering machine for stamping lines, this cushion is not necessary.

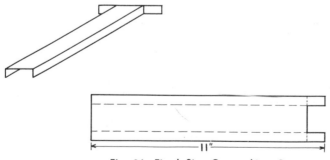

Fig. 36. Fixed Size Casemaking Gauge

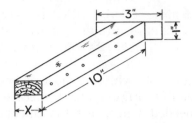

Fig. 37. Wood Casemaking Gauge

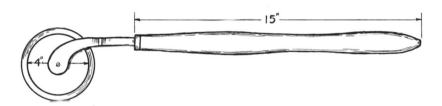

Fig. 38. Gold Roll

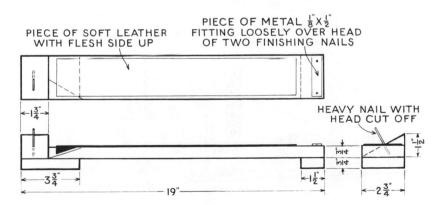

PIECE OF SOFT LEATHER
WITH FLESH SIDE UP

PIECE OF METAL $\frac{1}{8}"\times\frac{1}{2}"$
FITTING LOOSELY OVER HEAD
OF TWO FINISHING NAILS

HEAVY NAIL WITH
HEAD CUT OFF

Fig. 39. Roll-Gold Cushion

Fig. 40. Paper Cutter

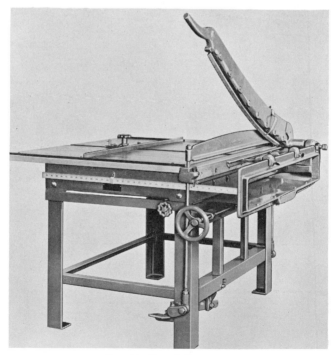

Fig. 41. Board Shears

Desirable Additional Equipment

In order to eliminate one of the most difficult hand tasks, that of cutting boards and materials for covers, a small *paper cutter* may be used, Figure 40.

For those having additional funds with which to equip a bindery, a *board shears*, Figure 41, should be purchased. A saving on this piece of equipment may be made if the bench shears alone is purchased and a suitable stand or table constructed, Figure 42. With it, all cutting problems will be solved except trimming edges of books.

If strength is of utmost importance to the workman in binding books, a stabbing machine, Figure 18, is probably the next most important piece of equipment. This machine or its equivalent saves time in that it punches all of the holes for overcasting, flat stitching, or the machine type of flat stitching. The stabber is also very accurate in punching holes, which makes for an easier job of sewing. A multiple-hole perforator or a multiple set of drills does a better job than punching, but these machines are quite expensive.

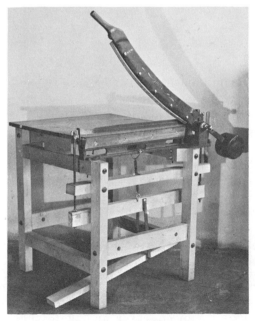

Fig. 42. Bench Shears

If the binder prefers ease of opening of books to strength, a stabber will be used only on books or magazines which are not in sections or for binding loose pages. In this case, a stabber would not be used very often, and another machine should be chosen that would be of more value to the binder.

In buying the next most necessary machine, one or two things must be considered. First, if there is no satisfactory way of lettering books, a *lettering machine,* Figure 43, should be purchased. If electric-pen lettering is satisfactory for the work to be done, a *cutting machine* for trimming the books would be more important. (See Figure 19.) If edges of the books are being sanded or a beveled chisel is being used satisfactorily, perhaps a *backer* should be purchased. Ordinarily, backing boards or a small wooden backer will not last long when used by a number of workers. When average hand equipment is already in use, it is recommended that the following machine equipment be purchased or made in this suggested order of importance:

1. Board shears (33"-45")
2. Stabber (perforator or drills—depending on types of sewing preferred)
3. Lettering machine
4. Cutting machine
5. Backer

If a lettering machine is purchased, one is confronted with the problem of selecting type. Because the type must be heated, it is recommended that brass type be purchased, as it will prove far superior to lead type, especially if it is used by a group of students or on many books. Lead type comes in a font of over 200 characters and costs about one-seventh as much as a 100-character font of brass type. The type may be purchased from any bindery or printing supply house. A condensed type of about 16- to 18-point size is recommended for an all-purpose size. If lower case can be purchased as well as capital letters, the workers can use the type to more advantage by putting the author in lower case and the title in capitals.

With school annuals or in any other situation where hundreds of covers will need to be stamped, a copper coated plate can be made by an engraver and plate shop. Covers may

Fig. 43. Lettering Machine

also be silk screened. Here the service of persons competent in design may be used.

Brass rule used for applying lines on the backs of books may also be purchased in inch lengths and should be cut into lengths which vary about $\frac{1}{8}''$, starting at $\frac{1}{2}''$ and stopping at about 3 inches. A single- or double-line rule may be used. This rule may also be purchased at any binders or printers supply house.

Again, individual requirements and interests will be the deciding factor in the selection of tools and equipment.

Chapter 4

Materials and Supplies

Most of the materials necessary for the binding of a book can be obtained at very little expense. This chapter discusses, compares and states where to purchase the materials.

Necessary Materials

The following materials and supplies or their substitutes are generally required:

1. Flexible bookbinders glue or paste
2. Joint strip material
3. Endsheet paper
4. Thread
5. Tapes and cords
6. Needles
7. Backing flannel
8. Headbands
9. Paper for spring backs
10. Flexible red board
11. Binders board
12. Cover materials
13. Lettering and finishing supplies
14. Book sizes and varnishes
15. Coach wadding
16. Ungummed holland tape or sign cloth
17. Glue brushes

Types of Glue

A flexible bookbinding glue will be found most satisfactory. Hard or flake glue, usually used in cabinet work, is
not satisfactory as it cracks when dry and causes the book to
break in the back and in the joints. Flexible glue may be purchased from any good bookbinders supply house. It may also
be ordered through a local printer. This glue comes in cakes
and is sold by the pound. It has glycerin and other ingredients
added to make it permanently flexible.

For the amateur who is experimenting, and for use with
certain types of work, a good flexible paste may be used. Paste
is as good as glue when prints and papers are used for cover
materials. If paste is used on the cover material, it should also
be used on the endsheets; otherwise the covers may warp. Glue,
rather than paste, should be used over the sewing on backs of
books. Paste may be secured from bindery supply houses, stationery stores, or may be made from the following formula:

PASTE

½ pound flour (2 cups)
1 teaspoon alum, mixed with the flour

Mix the flour with a little cold water, stirring to remove the lumps.
Add 8 cups of hot water and heat to a boil, stirring constantly. (This
mixture becomes partly clear when done.) Add ½ teaspoon oil of wintergreen (synthetic) or ½ teaspoon syrup of squills, which acts as a
preservative.

For all general use glue is superior to paste. Glue comes
from the manufacturer ready to use or in powderd form ready
to be dissolved in water. Flexible glue is used in a double boiler
or electric gluepot and should have water added until it is about
the consistency of thin syrup. A bit of experimenting will readily
produce the correct result.

Types of Glue Brushes

An important factor in the gluing process is the glue
brush. A round, copper-bound glue brush is best. These brushes
are made for this purpose and are more satisfactory than a
paint brush or other substitute. A 1-inch or 1½-inch size is
best for average size books. These brushes may be purchased
from any bindery supply house.

Endsheet Paper

A good grade of kraft paper is satisfactory for all endsheet requirements. This may be obtained from any good paper or stationery store or from a local printshop. It is available in several colors and the choice should be made in terms of the work to be done. This paper is manufactured so the fibers run in one direction, which lends additional strength when properly used.

Other wrapping papers may be substituted for the kraft paper, though they are usually not as strong. However, with the addition of a joint strip in endsheet make-up, they are quite satisfactory. Lightweight cover papers and heavy text papers may also be used as endsheets, provided they are not too stiff. The workman soon becomes "paper conscious" and is always on the alert for new kinds and colors which he may adapt to his use. Good grades of drawing paper can be colored to suit individual taste; they may also be marbled or tinted in a manner similar to the preparation of paper lamp shades. This is done by crumpling the paper as though it were to be thrown away. It is then smoothed out, and water colors or aniline dyes are used to color the paper. One color or several colors may be used to wash the paper. The colors become quite intense where the fibers of the paper have been broken or wrinkled. Practice will soon give the desired results.

Another method of "crinkling" the paper before dyeing it is to wrap a sheet around a broom handle and then force the two ends of the paper together. Do not wrap it around the handle too tightly.

Attractive endsheets may be made by using linoleum or wood-block prints on the paper. Stencils may be used with colors "sprayed" on the paper by means of a toothbrush dipped in different show-card colors and rubbed on a fine screen above the stencil.

Some bindery supply houses have special papers for endsheets of different colors which are very satisfactory. Construction paper, poster paper, and newsprint are not durable enough to be used as endsheets.

Material for Joint Strips

Joint strips have a distinct value in good bookbinding procedure. Two types of endsheet construction are detailed in the instruction units, one of which is the one-piece endsheet where the joint strip does not show. The best material for joint strips of this type is a special white drill cloth manufactured for this purpose, which may be purchased in 2-inch rolls (or in a roll 36 inches wide and then cut to 2-inch strips). Scraps of colored buckram may also be used for this purpose. On light-weight books, pieces of book cloth may be used, but it is not as satisfactory as buckram or drill cloth. Coated fabric should never be used as a joint strip when one-piece endsheets are used, as the glue will not stick to the endsheet at the joint.

Where the binder prefers a two-piece endsheet and the joint strip is to show, buckram should be used. This is true especially on heavy volumes. This material may be bought in 2-inch rolls, or scraps of buckram may be used. Scraps of book cloth may be used as joint strips on small books. Care in selecting a joint strip to match the cover will add to the attractiveness of the finished book. In dry climates, joint strips made of coated fabric may be used in making up the two-piece endsheet but are not satisfactory in areas having high humidity.

Types of Thread

The craftsman has a choice between three kinds of thread — cotton, nylon, or linen. While cotton thread may be used, it deteriorates rapidly and lacks the strength of linen and nylon.

Wherever possible, a good *linen* thread should be used. This may be purchased in ½-pound spools. Smaller spools may be secured from any bindery supply house or at some dry-goods stores. The natural color is preferred. Sizes range from No. 12 to No. 32, with No. 12 being the heavier. Most commonly used are sizes 12-4, 16-3, and 20-2; and if only one kind is to be used for all books, No. 16-3 is recommended. Where much binding is to be done, a variety of sizes should be secured in order to meet the requirements of varying section and book sizes.

Nylon is very strong and durable, but it does not have the "life" or "give" of linen. Also, it is easier to pull it so tightly that the sheets are cut by the thread.

Tapes and Cords

The cords used in loom sewing (sometimes called "kettle cords") are listed by most supply houses as soft twine and may be secured in ½-pound balls. Any strong, soft twine which can be frayed may be substituted. The binder may do all of his sewing using cords if tapes are not available. This will be discussed in Part Two.

Binding tapes come in several widths. The ½-inch width is the best for all general use and may be purchased in 36-yard rolls at bindery supply houses or dry-goods stores. The heaviest of the tapes used in dressmaking will serve as a satisfactory substitute.

Types of Needles

In overcast sewing, it is necessary to sew through sections where holes are not punched and a sharp needle must be used. A 1/0 harness needle is satisfactory. If needles of this kind are purchased, they may also be used for lacing purposes in leatherwork. Needles may be obtained at any dry goods store, or bindery supply house.

Reinforcing Material

After a book is sewed, it is recommended that some kind of reinforcing material be glued on the back edge to keep the sections more rigid while trimming, and to make rounding and backing easier. The advantage of this procedure before rounding and backing will be appreciated if both approaches are experienced. A strong material which will stretch readily and yet not break is required. A good grade of outing flannel will prove satisfactory. All dry-goods stores have outing flannel and any color may be used, as it will not show when the book is completed.

The flannel should have its warp and weft running diagonally across the cloth instead of at right angles to the edges. Outing flannel should be cut diagonally instead of straight across the piece.

Bindery supply houses have a medium-weight backing flannel which looks like heavy muslin on one side and has a flannel finish on the other and is probably the most satisfactory to use. Muslin makes a fair reinforcing material for small books and school annuals, but it is not recommended for general use, although its cost is less than flannel.

Super cloth (a sized cheesecloth) is too light for reinforcing purposes if strength is a primary consideration.

Headbands

Headbands are not absolutely necessary in the binding of a book, although they do make a more attractive volume. They may be secured from any bindery supply house or made from silk, cotton, mercerized prints, broadcloth, or other material. The workman may make his own by following this procedure:

1. Cut 1-inch strips from the material and paste or lightly glue them on one side.

2. Place a piece of grocery twine so that it divides the 1-inch strip in two, lengthwise, Figure 44.

3. Fold one edge over the string and rub with a bone folder so the cord is forced up on one side, Figure 45.

4. These strips are ready to use when dry.

Take care to combine the colors of headbands and cover materials effectively.

Materials for Spring Backs

While a lightweight wrapping paper will work satisfactorily for spring backs, the lightweight kraft paper is best. The heavier weight of this paper was described and recommended for endsheet use. It can be secured at almost any stationery store, printshop, or paper supply company.

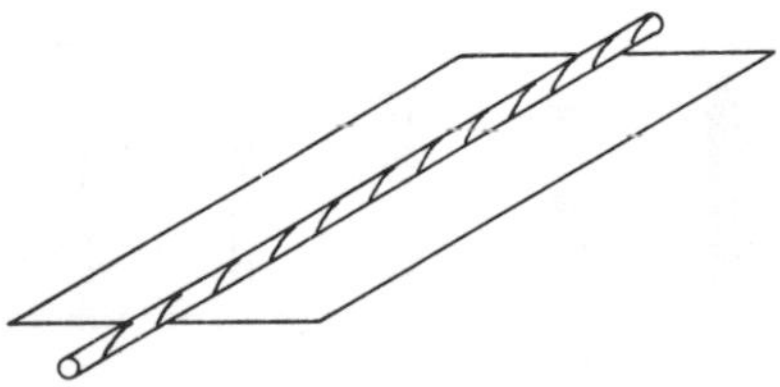

Fig. 44. Placement of Twine
in Making Headbands

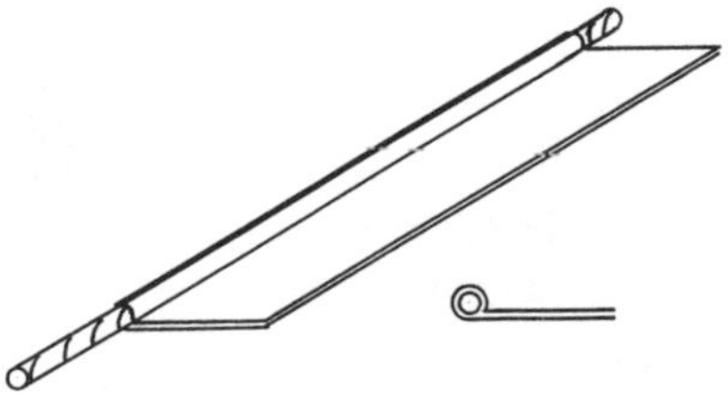

Fig. 45. Completed Headband

Boards for Covers

Many kinds of boards may be obtained for cover use. A regular *binders board* is the best, although, in emergency situations, substitutes may have to be used. Binders board may be secured from any paper supply house in 50-pound bundles or purchased in single pieces. Common sizes are 26″ x 38″ and 22″ x 28″, and thickness is determined by the number of 26″ x 38″ boards to the bundle. The most used boards are No. 20 and No. 15 (26″ x 38″ basic size); following this rule there would be twenty No. 20 boards to the bundle and fifteen of No. 15. It will readily be seen that No. 15 board is the heavier of the two. In the average binding work, No. 12 will probably be the heaviest board needed and No. 25 the lightest. These four weights, then, would meet almost any purpose. Binders working with hand equipment should avoid No. 12. An occasional need for a heavy board may be met by gluing two No. 25 boards together.

For convenience, Figure 46 summarizes the weights of boards and their original sizes. The two common sizes mentioned in the instruction sheets in this book are C (No. 15) and D (No. 20) board and are based on the 26″ x 38″ size. If a binder

BINDERS-BOARD CHART

Size	Number					
20 x 30	17	19	25	35	40	50
22 x 28	17	19	25	35	40	50
24 x 36	12	14	18	25	29	36
26 x 38	10	12	15	20	25	30
33 x 44	7	8	11	15	17	21
Code (as used in this book)	A	B	C	D	E	F
Gauge or thickness in thousandths	.145	.125	.098	.070	.060	.045
Actual thickness of board						

Fig. 46. Binders Board Chart

finds it more convenient to buy boards in the 20″ x 30″size and wants the No. 15 board specified here, he should order No. 25 in order to get the same thickness; if he buys his stock in 22″ x 28″ pieces and wants the thickness of the No. 20 board specified in this book, he must buy No. 35.

Binders board is harder and tougher than most materials which may be used for cover stock. However, if a substitute is mandatory, *pasted chipboard* can be used. Chipboard is softer than binders board and tends to separate into thin layers when dropped on the corners. More than one-third of the cost may be saved when chipboard is selected over binders board, but strength and durability are sacrificed.

Cardboard used in window-display advertising may be secured from stores and used for covers. Dry-goods stores also are sources of cover stock when large displays have served their purpose. While these boards are soft they work well as substitutes. *Do not attempt to use corrugated cardboard.*

Sometimes the cover material can be removed from old used covers and the boards may be trimmed for use on smaller books. Occasionally the board may be used again on the same book if the corners are not "soft." Usually, this is not considered good practice.

In books requiring a padded cover, always use *flexible redboard,* covered with *coach wadding and super cloth or muslin.* Redboard may be purchased at any reliable paper supply house. Coach wadding is a dark, blue-black padding material and may be purchased at any upholstering supply house.

Cover Materials

The binder of a book should always be aware of materials and methods which make for both strength and durability. Assuming that a book will have considerable use, coated fabrics, vinyl, or impregnated buckram are recommended for binding material. (See page 22, list of Standard Binding Fabrics.)

Coated fabric is available under many trade names, produced by a number of manufacturers. It is a waterproof binding material which may be secured in many colors, patterns and "grains." The library weight is best for all common purposes although it may be secured in both lighter and heavier weights.

Buckram is especially strong. The waterproof finish is recommended because the regular finish spots easily. After the buckram bindings have been varnished, they seem to outwear coated-fabric bindings in humid climates.

Book cloth is a lightweight material made from cotton with a filler added to give it "body." The pyroxylin-impregnated varieties are waterproof and may be obtained in several colors and patterns.

Coated fabrics, buckram, and book cloth may be purchased in several widths (30" to 48") by the yard or in forty- to sixty-yard rolls. A few large department stores stock them, but a greater choice is possible when orders are sent directly to bindery supply houses.

Print goods, oilcloth, corduroy, or other substitute materials may be secured at any department store.

For books requiring leather cover material, library morocco (goat) or pigskin may be purchased from a bindery supply house or a leather company. It is sold by the skin and is priced by the square foot. All colors are available. For Bibles, a *levant grain morocco* is recommended; this material is sometimes called *Bible Morocco.*

Cowhides are occasionally used for binding and a regular library cowhide may be obtained in a variety of colors for this purpose. Cowhides are sold by the "side," which is half of a regular hide.

Materials for Lettering

The lettering problem is a simple one if titles are put on with pen and ink. All that is required is a waterproof ink of suitable color and a lettering pen. Flexible book varnish, obtainable at a bindery supply house, is usually applied over the ink. Clear laquer is sometimes substituted for the book varnish. Shellac is not desirable because it tends to turn white on the cover material.

Lettering may be done by hand with an electric pen and decorative foil. Foil may be purchased in many colors in addition to gold and aluminum. Book varnish is applied over the foil to prevent oxidation. Foil may be readily purchased in 200-foot rolls, 1" and 2" wide. It is also available in sheets. For economy and ease of handling, a roll about 2 inches wide is recommended. Gold is the most popular color.

If a lettering machine is used, the foil mentioned in the preceding paragraph will meet all requirements. Gold leaf (23 carat) may also be used but is quite expensive. It may be secured from a bindery supply house in 100-foot rolls and in sheets 3¼" square. This 23-carat gold foil is more than four times as expensive as the imitation gold foil. *Pure gold should always be used on leather, as imitation gold tarnishes.*

If a hand pallet is used, gold leaf must be purchased unmounted in "books." These sheets are about 3" x 4".

Some fabrics are sized for lettering in the manufacturing process. On others, the back of the book should be "sized" before any kind of lettering is done so that the gold or foil will adhere to the material. An exception to this would be the use of a paper label on a gingham-covered cookbook. For starch-filled fabrics or leather-bound books, an egg size should be used. For coated fabrics and vinyls, not pre-sized for lettering, a commercial size is recommended. The binder may choose to make his own from one of the following formulas for use on untreated buckrams or leather:

EGG SIZE

white of 1 egg
1 teaspoon white vinegar

Mix the egg white and vinegar with a small beater and let stand for 12 to 18 hours. Strain through a fine cloth. For a preservative, add a few drops of syrup of squills. If sizing should thicken, add a little warm water to thin it.

EGG ALBUMEN SIZE

½ pint of warm water
1 teaspoonful of Borax
pinch of oxalic acid crystals
pinch of sal ammoniac
3 teaspoons of oil of wintergreen (synthetic)
5 tablespoons of egg albumen
1 tablespoon of blood albumen

Add ingredients to warm water. Stir two or three times within twenty-four (24) hours. Leave sediment in bottom of container.

When ready to use, pour out a small amount of the egg size in a small jar and add one teaspoonful of syrup of squills, for a preservative.

Put lard on the sponge to be used in applying the sizing. This keeps the sponge from frothing.

Coated or impregnated fabrics may be sized with one of the patented sizes or a size may be prepared from the following formula:

ADHESIVE COATING AND COATED FABRIC LETTERING SIZE[1]

equal parts orange shellac and alcohol
¼ part of household ammonia
¼ part ethyl acetate

Reduce with alcohol to fairly thin consistency.

[1] From A. B. Seaver, Denver, Colorado.

Chapter 5

Binding Books by Machine

This book you hold in your hands didn't just happen. It represents the combined work of authors, editors, typesetters, proofreaders and printers whose efforts culminate with the binders. The paper used originated in a forest and was helped to perfection by the paper chemist. Another individual designed the type used, while still others fabricated the cover material. Add to these the contributions of persons engaged in packaging, transportation, and sales and you have an idea of the people behind the production and sale of a book.

A Brief History

Books originally were produced entirely by hand, from the processing of the parchment sheet to the hand lettering and illumination, and on to hand binding. Countless hours were spent on a single volume. No one should ever pass up the opportunity to view the ancient manuscripts now preserved in museums and private collections.

Antedating the book, as we think of it today, records were kept on stone and clay tablets. Walls of temples still bear the messages of the ages. The scroll of papyrus is a type of book and the manner in which they are rolled for storage can be thought of as a form of "binding."

Members of monastic orders produced the complete book, from the hand lettering and illumination of the page to the fine leather binding. Books of the period were large and the covers provided a spacious surface for embellishment. Even the back of the book lent itself to design. As originally produced, books were true works of art, each unique, each containing the written record of man's thinking.

Through the years we have witnessed a step-by-step improvement in tools, machines, and equipment for the production of books. New materials have been introduced. But with all the changes, the *basic* steps of binding a book have remained the same. Just as the monk started with the pages of parchment, so does the modern binder start with what he calls "sheetwork." This begins with the receipt of the printed pages and includes folding, endsheeting, tipping, gathering, sewing, and smashing. Second in the series of steps in the production of the book is "forwarding." Processes here are back gluing, trimming, rounding, backing and lining. The third and last of the basic steps is called "finishing." Here we find the making of cases, stamping of the covers, and casing in. All this is done carefully, accurately, and very rapidly in the modern commercial bindery.

In the beginning of the development of bookbinding, the product was large and bulky due to the need for rather big sheets which could accept a considerable amount of lettering done laboriously by hand. The parchment sheets themselves were reasonably thick, and the boards and leather of the cover were still proportionately thicker. Through the years man has created new materials and new processes, and bookbinding along with many other areas of manufacturing has received the benefits of the industrial revolution.

There are many who feel that when a product is *machine made* it has sacrificed both quality and character. This is not true. No machine has ever had a part in *deciding* on the construction of an object, its design, or the quality of the material used. That is man's job, and what man *wants to do* he can achieve with the aid of a machine developed for the purpose. Thus we see that when you have a good book in your hands, its quality is high because it was planned that way. Good grades of paper and cover material were selected, and the several steps of binding were planned to insure strength and durability. A designer had a major hand in the plan and his thinking is reflected in the end papers used, the color and texture of the cover material, and the choice and placement of type selected to designate the title and author of the volume. Good quality can be achieved with machines. Granted that a "hand-bound" volume has a quality all its own, a book produced by machine can also be strong, well designed, and a source of pride to a critical owner. What man *wants,* man can produce by hand or by machine if he is willing to assume the cost.

Just as automobiles, refrigerators, and television sets have been adapted to the assembly line in order to reduce their production cost, so have machines been developed to produce good books in order that all of us may have personal libraries at a reasonable cost.

The first chapters of this volume presented basic information about the parts of a book, the equipment for binding, and the materials used. In order to complete an understanding of bookbinding, it is fitting to look at how industry meets the challenge of producing millions of volumes each year, ranging from the inexpensive paperback on to the finest of books. Experience in hand bookbinding will help us appreciate the excellent work that can be done with machines.

Importance of Bookbinding

Books have always been the symbol of the cultured, educated, well-informed individual. The content of books seems to range without limit, from the first grader's beginning reader to prized volumes published in limited editions. There are anthologies, biographies, novels, poetry, treatises on the space age, how-to-do-it, travel, stamp collecting—the list of subjects would be endless.

The great demand for books in all price ranges has caused the expansion of bookbinding as a major industry. Originally the last step in the production of a single volume, binding moved to the commercial printshop and from there to the independent role it plays today. Here automation makes its contribution to the book reading public.

The Printed Sheets

The book originates with large sheets of printed pages which are folded into *signatures*. What will be a 16-page section is folded from a sheet with 8 printed pages to a side, arranged according to a predetermined *imposition* (folding plan). The sheet becomes a section in a folding machine, Figure 47. There are two types of folding machines: (1) the buckle and (2) the tape and knife. The knife folder will accommodate a bulky final fold, as in a 64-page signature. The buckle fold machine is used for small forms and has the ability to fold at right angles, parallel, or a combination of both. Following the folding the sections are jogged, bundled and made ready for gathering.

Fig. 47. Four-Section Buckle Folder with Continuous Feed, Capable of Handling 39" x 52" Sheets (Courtesy, Baumfolder)

Attaching Endsheets

Endsheets are applied by an automatic tipping machine which pastes the folded sheets on the outside of the first and last signatures.

When a book is to contain pictures, maps or illustrations which were not printed on the regular pages, a special "tipping" operation is necessary. This adds to the cost of the volume because it must be done by hand. If the picture is to appear inside a signature, the problem becomes even more complicated. Here again we can understand the "design" problem that lies back of the production of a book.

Gathering the Signatures

Assembling the sections in a sequence that will make the complete book is called *gathering*. This is accomplished in to-day's modern bindery by a gathering machine, Figure 48. The old hand process is almost duplicated in this machine. Signa-

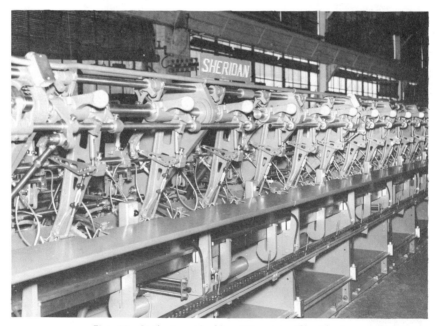

Fig. 48. Gathering Machine (Courtesy, Sheridan)

tures are removed from hoppers by gripper fingers, as contrast-
ed with the hand method of picking from stacks placed along
the edge of a table.

Sewing the Books

Books are sewed on two different kinds of machines,
Figure 49. A book whose sections have been Smyth sewed will

Fig. 49. Smyth Book Sewing Machine (Courtesy, Smyth)

open page by page to the back of the section. Cotton or nylon thread is used, and from 4,000 to 6,000 signatures may be sewed per hour.

Another type of sewing is used on school texts and other books which are subject to hard usage. The process here is called side sewing and the operation is performed on a machine similar to that used by every dressmaker. However, it takes longer stitches and can accommodate books up to ¾″ thick. The sewing itself takes place after the signatures have been wire stitched in a machine synchronized to the gathering process. When a book is thicker than ¾″, it is usually drilled and sewed on a heavier machine designed for the purpose.

Trimming the Books

Here the second phase of binding, called forwarding, starts. Glue is applied to the back of the book to secure the sections firmly. In this process each book passes a roller of the gluing machine. When the backs have become dry, books are gathered in small bundles and are trimmed on three edges in one continuous operation.

Fig. 50. Forwarding Machine (Courtesy, Book Machinery)

Rounding, Backing, and Lining

Automatic bookbinding machines are seen at their best as they perform the processes of *forwarding*. See Figure 50. Two types of forwarding machines exist, each doing the same type of work though by different methods. In each machine the back of the book is pulled into a round shape following which a rocking iron forms the joint. The back of the book then receives a coating of flexible glue and a piece of stiff "super" cloth is applied. This gauze-like material misses the top and bottom of the book about ½ inch and extends over the sides about 1 inch. The back receives another coat of flexible glue, and a crash paper lining to which headbands have been attached is applied to make sure that they stick properly.

Cutting Cover Boards

A little later as a final step in the binding process we shall see the "casing in" operation. This case, or *cover*, will consist of the cover material itself, the front and back boards, and the strip called the *backbone*. A hand bookbinder may refer to the backbone as the lettering strip.

Fig. 51. End Feed Casemaker with Tandem Glue and Strip Feed Unit
(Courtesy, Sheridan)

Most commercial binderies use a power rotary cutter for cutting the binders board. Sheets are first cut to the correct length followed by a second feeding which produces the desired width.

Making Covers

Book covers, known in the trade as *cases*, are made by two different types of casemaking machines, Figure 51. One uses pre-cut pieces of cover material. These were cut (by machine) to the size of the finished case plus a ⅝" allowance for a turn-in on the four edges. The prescribed design or lettering may have been printed on the cover material before covers are made. Lithographed or silk screened covers are usually printed on the cloth before making the case. After a time allowance for drying, these imprinted pieces of cover material, the boards which will become the front and back covers and the material for the back lining are all placed in the casemaking machine.

Automatically the cover boards and back lining are positioned on the glued cover material, the corners are cut, and the edges turned. The case is then run through a set of rollers to smooth out wrinkles and eliminate air pockets. This particular type of casemaking machine is used for short runs and pre-printed cover material.

The other type of casemaking machine uses a continuous roll of cover material previously cut to either the length or width of the cover. As the material is drawn forward, glue is applied to it and the cover boards and back lining are dropped into position, corner cutters remove excess cloth, the cover material is turned over on two sides, the case is cut from the roll and the other two sides turned. The case is then sent between rollers that remove wrinkles and press out air pockets. It is now ready for stamping or other treatment determined in the original design of the book.

Stamping Book Covers

Cover treatment ranges from simple gold lettering to elaborate designs which employ a generous use of color. Some machines use the printing technique with ink as a medium, while others use brass dies and heat to set one of the several foils available. See Figure 52. Pure gold leaf will always maintain its position at the top of the list of quality materials. Chromium-plated brass dies are used in long runs because they are harder and last longer. Where just a few covers are involved, individual type may be used.

Casing-In the Books

A bindery will use two types of casing-in machines, the *wing* and the *semiautomatic*, with the wing being the more common. This type has three wings evenly spaced on a cylinder. As each wing moves into position, the feeder places a completely forwarded book astride it. The winged book is revolved below two paste boxes which will paste the endsheets. The finished case is moved to a spot directly above the book, the wing moves

Fig. 52. Embossing Press (Courtesy, Sheridan)

the book up, the endsheets are pasted and the cover falls into place. The wing turns another one-third revolution and the operator removes the book and makes any necessary adjustment before placing the volume on boards for a final pressing.

Fig. 53. Casing-In Machine (Courtesy, Smyth)

When the semi-automatic machine is employed for ca₁ the book enters at the bottom and constantly works its ⱴ upward. Following the pasting of the endsheets and the application of the cover, the volume slides down a chute to the operator for inspection and adjustment, Figure 53. The books are placed between brass-bound boards and taken to a hydraulic press where they remain until dry.

After being removed from the press, the books are given a final inspection, a plain or printed book jacket is placed over the covers, and the books are wrapped in packages and packed for shipment to the publisher's warehouse.

Another story could be told about binding books by machine with the recently developed "perfect binders." These machines are made both in Europe and the United States and use adhesives in place of threads for "sewing." The speed of

Fig. 54. Perfect Binder (Courtesy, Sheridan)

these machines is tremendous, turning out books with paper covers at the rate of 200 per minute, Figure 54. The machine can also be adapted to case hard-covered books. The miracles of invention and mechanization are apparent on every hand as one visits a modern commercial bindery.

A tremendous amount of thinking and planning goes into every book. Would that all consumers of books could fully understand and appreciate what it takes to put a volume on the library shelf!

Part II

Bookbinding Processes

This second part presents step-by-step procedure in the binding of all types of books. These processes as they appear are the result of many years of experimentation in the teaching of high-school and college classes. In addition to their use in public schools, several librarians, teachers of adult education classes, and home craftsmen have found them most valuable.

Processes 1 to 27 include procedure for full binding; Processes 28 to 35 present procedures for quarter-, half, and three-quarter binding. It will be noticed that Processes 1 to 19 are identical in all types of bindings and are not repeated in the instructions for quarter-, half-, and three-quarter bindings. The workman in his use of these processes should follow one of two procedures, depending upon the type of book he is binding.

A. When binding full-bound books, use Procedures 1 through 28.

B. When binding half-, quarter-, or three-quarter-bound books, use Processes 1 through 19 and Processes 28 through 35. (Here Processes 20 to 28 are omitted because they apply only to full bindings.)

As was explained in Part One, the only difference between quarter-, half-, and three-quarter binding is in the distance that the material on the back extends over the sides of the book, and in the size of the corners. Half-binding is the most commonly used. Specific instruction for cutting material for quarter- and three-quarter-bound books is listed in Process 28, and the procedure of applying material in all three types is the same.

Two charts with the step-by-step procedure of the hand binding process follow. These should prove useful both to students in classes and the individual working at home as a hobby.

73

Sequence of Processes
(By types of sewing, with use of joint strips)

For Books That Do Not Have To Be Resewn	Flat or Machine Stitch	Overcast Stitch
1	2	3
1. Enter book on record card. (p. 149)	1. Enter book on record card. (p. 149)	1. Enter book on record card. (p. 149)
2. CUT TWO END-SHEETS same length as book, but twice as wide plus ¼". (p. 82)	2. CUT ENDSHEETS: Cut 4 endsheets the same size of book. (pp. 82-85)	2. CUT ENDSHEETS: Cut 4 endsheets the same size of book. (pp. 82-85)
3. FOLD and APPLY endsheets making sure fold comes flush with back edge of book. (p. 82)	3. CUT JOINT STRIPS: Cut 2 joint strips 2" wide and the length of the book. (p. 83)	3. CUT JOINT STRIPS: Cut 2 joint strips 2" wide and the length of the book. (p. 83)
4. CUT and APPLY backing flannel 2½" wide plus width of back edge of book. (p. 82)	4. MAKE UP ENDSHEETS. (pp. 83-84) 5. PUNCH BOOK. (p. 88) 6. SEW THE BOOK. (pp. 93-97) 7. TURN BACK the joint strips over the sewing. (p. 103)	4. MAKE UP ENDSHEETS. (pp. 83-84) 5. PUNCH BOOK. (p. 88) 6. SEW THE BOOK. (pp. 93-97) 7. TURN BACK the joint strips over the sewing. (p. 103)
5. TRIM book if necessary 1. Front 2. Bottom 3. Top (pp. 106-107)	8. CHECK THE PAGING. (p. 104) 9. APPLY BACKING FLANNEL. (p. 105) 10. TRIM the book: 1. Front, 2. Bottom, 3. Top. (pp. 106-107)	8. CHECK THE PAGING. (p. 104) 9. APPLY BACKING FLANNEL. (p. 105) 10. TRIM the book: 1. Front, 2. Bottom, 3. Top. (pp. 106-107)
6. ROUND THE BOOK. (p. 109)	11. BACK THE book a small amount. (p. 111)	11. ROUND THE BOOK. (p. 109) 12. BACK the book. (p. 111)
7. BACK THE BOOK. (p. 111)	12. CUT COVERS: ¼" longer than book; flush on the front edge when pushed into the joint made by backing. (pp. 117-118)	13. APPLY the headbands. (p.112) 14. APPLY the spring back. (pp. 112-116)
8. APPLY the headbands. (p.112)		
9. APPLY the spring back. (pp. 112-116)	13. CUT LETTER-ING strip the length of cover and the width of the back edge. (p. 119)	15. CUT COVERS: ¼" longer than book; flush on the front edge when pushed into the joint made by backing. (pp. 117-118)
10. CUT covers: ¼" longer than book; flush on the front edge when pushed into the joint made by backing. (pp. 117-118)	14. Have instructor check size of covers and lettering strip.	
11. CUT lettering strip the length of the covers and the width of the back edge. (p. 119)		16. CUT LETTER-ING strip the length of the covers and the width of back edge. (p. 119)
12. Have instructor check size of covers and lettering strip.		17. Have instructor check size of covers and lettering strip.

74

Loom Sewing	Saddle Stitch
4	5

Loom Sewing	Saddle Stitch
1. Enter book on record card. (p. 149)	1. Enter book on record card. (p. 149)
2. CUT ENDSHEETS: Two ½" wider than book; two ½" narrower than book; all four the same length of book. (pp. 85-86)	2. CUT ENDSHEETS: Cut one same length, twice as wide, plus ½". Cut 2 more same size as the book. (p. 86)
3. CUT TWO JOINT strips 2" wide and length of the book. (p. 85)	
4. MAKE UP ENDSHEETS: making sure to fasten joint strip to smallest endsheet. (pp. 85-86)	3. CUT JOINT STRIPS: One 2" wide and length of book. (p. 86)
5. SAW OUT SECTIONS in finishers clamp. (pp. 89-92)	4. MAKE UP ENDSHEETS. (pp. 86-87)
6. APPLY ENDSHEETS to back of front section, and front of back section. (pp. 91-92)	5. APPLY ENDSHEETS. (p. 87)
7. APPLY gummed holland tape down center of first and last sections. (Fig. 57)	6. PUNCH pamphlet in V-trough. (p. 93)
8. PUNCH through tape and joint strips in V-trough (p. 01)	7. SEW THE BOOK. (pp. 101-103)
9. SET UP LOOM. (p. 97)	8. CHECK paging. (p. 104)
10. SEW BOOK. (pp. 97-101)	9. GLUE on ¾" strip of backing flannel. (p. 105)
11. CUT BOOK OFF of loom. (p. 100)	10. TRIM the book:
12. GLUE DOWN "slips." (p. 100)	1. Front
13. CHECK PAGING. (p. 104)	2. Bottom
14. APPLY BACKING flannel. (p. 105)	3. Top
15. TRIM THE BOOK. (pp. 106-107)	(pp. 106-107)
16. ROUND THE BOOK. (p. 109)	11. CUT COVERS: ¼" longer than book, in ⅛" on back edge of book and flush with front edge. (pp. 117-118)
17. BACK THE BOOK. (p. 111)	
18. APPLY HEADBANDS if necessary. (p. 112)	12. Have instructor check size of covers.
19. APPLY SPRING back. (pp. 112-116)	
20. CUT COVERS: same size as for other kinds of books. (pp. 117-118)	
21. CUT LETTERING strip. (p. 119)	

Full-Binding Processes	Half-Binding Processes (Composite)

1. CUT BINDING materials. (pp. 118-119)
2. MAKE UP COVERS. (pp. 119-121)
  a. Glue back cover and place on binding material. (Fig. 81, p. 120)
  b. Place book on back cover with ⅛" square on front edge. (p. 118)
  c. Glue front cover, and place on book (glued side up) with ⅛" front square.
  d. Draw over binding material on to front cover.
  e. Have instructor check your cover.
3. APPLY LETTERING STRIP. (p. 121)
4. TURN IN EDGES. Turn top and bottom edges first. (p. 122)
5. LETTER COVER and apply lines. (pp. 124-129)
6. CHECK LETTERING. (pp. 128-129)
7. HANG IN BOOK. (p. 129)
8. GLUE UP ENDSHEETS. (pp. 129-130)
9. PRESS BOOK. (pp. 130-131)
10. CLEAN UP BOOK. (p. 131)
11. RUBBER STAMP name of binder on inside of next to last back endsheet.
12. VARNISH over lettering and back binding material. (p. 133)
	1. SPACE out lettering strip for bands. (Fig. 70, p. 15)
	2. APPLY bands to lettering strip. (p. 138)
	3. CUT BACK STRIP: 2" longer than covers and 3½" plus the width of the back edge of the book. (If book is to have a half-goat binding, cut the back strip from Library Morocco goat.) (p. 135)
	4. CUT FOUR pieces of material for corners. (If book is to have a half-goat binding, cut the corners from Library Morocco goat.) (p. 137)
	5. PARE OR SKIVE ALL THE EDGES OF the corners and the back piece, if you are using leather for the binding material. (p. 139)
	6. APPLY THE FOUR corners. (p. 139)
	7. APPLY BACK STRIP to covers, being sure that a larger square allowance was made on the front edge than on the top and bottom edges. (p. 140)
	8. APPLY LETTERING STRIP: Rub out bands if leather is used. (p. 141)
	9. LETTER COVER. (pp. 141-143)
	10. CHECK LETTERING. (pp. 128-129)
	11. TURN IN "heads" of cover. (pp. 143-144)
	12. HANG IN book. (p. 144)
	13. CUT SIDING UP material. (pp. 145-146)
	14. APPLY SIDING UP material. (pp. 145-146)
	15. GLUE UP ENDSHEETS. (p. 146)
	16. PRESS BOOK. (pp. 130-131)
	17. CLEAN UP BOOK and identify binder by placing rubber stamp on inside of next to last back endsheet.
	18. ROLL gold lines on book. (p. 147)
	19. VARNISH over lettering and back binding material. (p. 147)

Quarter-Binding Processes
(Composite)

1. CUT BACK STRIP: 2" longer than covers and 3½" plus the width of the back edge of the book. (p. 135)
2. PARE OR SKIVE the edges of the back piece, if you are using leather for the back piece. (p. 139)
3. APPLY BACK STRIP to covers, being sure that a square was allowed on the front edge equal to the square on the top and bottom edges. (p. 140) (Have instructor check your cover at this point.)
4. APPLY LETTERING STRIP. (p. 121)
5. LETTER COVER and apply lines. (pp. 124-129)
6. CHECK LETTERING. (pp. 128-129)
7. TURN IN "heads" of cover. (pp. 143-144)
8. HANG IN BOOK. (p. 144)
9. CUT SIDING UP. (pp. 145-146)
10. APPLY SIDING UP. (p. 146)
11. GLUE UP ENDSHEETS. (pp. 129-130)
12. PRESS BOOK. (pp. 130-131)
13. CLEAN UP BOOK. (p. 131)
14. RUBBER STAMP name of binder on inside of next to last back endsheet.
15. VARNISH over lettering and back binding material. (p. 147)

Chapter 6

Making Up and Applying Endsheets

Process 1. Preparing the Contents for Binding

Materials and Equipment

Mending tape (transparent)
Cutting knife
Oyster knife
Backing hammer
Pliers

Removing Covers and Inspecting a Book to be Rebound

If the book is to be rebound, the covers must be removed by using a knife to cut the endsheets loose at the joint. This process should be carried through very carefully because the instructions of the owner may specify "rebind in old cover." After the cover has been removed, the old glue can be loosened from the back by pounding with the backing hammer and scraping with the oyster knife. If the sewing is loose or if there are some loose sections, the book must be "torn down" or separated into sections or signatures by using the knife to cut the old sewing. However, if the sewing on the book is still good, there is no reason to tear it down.

Preparing Magazines for Binding

If a volume of magazines is to be bound, be careful to follow the owner's directions. If the instructions say "strip cover," "strip covers and ads," or "bind all," they must be carried out. If the magazines are stapled together, use the oyster knife or staple extractor and pliers to remove the staples. By using the backing hammer and pounding the back of each magazine, the glue will be loosened, and it will be easy to tear it down into sections. Lay the book flat on the desk and strike along the top edge of the back to loosen the glue.

Generally the *Title Page, Index,* and *Table of Contents* are in the last number of the set of magazines. The *Title Page* will always be bound in the front of the volume. If the *Index* and *Table of Contents* are in small Roman numerals, such as *i, ii, iii, iv,* they are to be bound in the front immediately following the *Title Page.* If the pages of the *Index* are numbered consecutively in Arabic numbers, such as *298, 299, 300, 301,* they of course will remain where they are in the magazine. There are a few exceptions to the above rules. Some magazines do not bind the *Title Page, Index* or *Table of Contents* in a regular issue, and they must be obtained from the publisher. Sometimes the *Index* and *Table of Contents* are not numbered, and in such instances they are bound in the front of the magazines.

Minor Repair Work

After the books or magazines have been torn down, it is advisable to patch torn places with a transparent tape or fibrous Japanese tissue paper. Generally an application of tape or tissue on one side is sufficient, but if necessary the tape may be applied on both sides of the torn page. Use the regular transparent adhesive tape which is made especially for mending torn pages. Avoid heavy weights of tape.

The type of sewing and the kind of sheets to be used should now be determined.

Process 2. Determining Type of Sewing to be Used

Applying Double Endsheets Without Resewing

If the sewing on the book is still good—no loose sections or loose pages—the endsheets may be cut as shown in Process 3.

The sewing of books which have not been rebound since leaving the publishers can be tested by locating the center of any section and snapping the threads with the fingernail to see if the sewing has "life." If the threads snap back in place, the sewing is in good condition and the book does not need to be torn down; however, if the threads do not snap back into place, the sewing must be cut and the book torn into sections. If the sewing is in good condition, double endsheets are cut and applied as shown in Process 3.

The "Sewing-On-Endsheets" Method

This method of fastening endsheets may be used on books whose sewing is still good, but it will not prove to be as satisfactory as cutting a double endsheet as outlined in Process 3. Test the sewing before selecting this type of sewing on endsheets. Methods of cutting and applying the endsheets are shown in Process 4.

Flat Stitching

If the book is less than ½" thick and has wide margins, it should be flat stitched unless it is a volume which must lie flat when open. Follow instructions in Process 4 for the procedure in cutting endsheets for flat stitching. Books made up of single sheets must be flat stitched. Books originally in sections but which now have many loose single pages should be flat stitched. Books made up of sections which have very narrow margins should be loom sewed if possible.

Machine Stitching

If a book is 1" or less in thickness and has wide margins, it should be machine stitched. The endsheets are cut the same as for the flat-stitched book. See Process 4.

Overcast Sewing

Any book which is more than 1" in thickness is generally sewed by the overcast method, provided the pages have good margins and the book does not have to lie flat when open. When cutting endsheets for overcast-sewed books, follow Process 4.

Nailing

Occasionally a very large book with wide margins, but with many small sections, needs an unusual type of fastening. Nailing the book is probably the strongest type of fastening in this case. This method of fastening is used on tax schedules, thick check books, and some newspaper bindings. Thick books which have many thin sections, but do not need to be rounded or backed, may be fastened together by this method. Cut and make up the endsheets as shown in Process 4.

Loom Sewing

Books whose pages are in sections with narrow margins are generally sewed on the loom or "sewing frame." Books which are to lie flat when open should also be sewed in this manner. Loom sewing is not a strong type of sewing, but it does have an important place in binding. Most music books and Bibles are sewed in this way. For cutting endsheets for this type of sewing see Process 5.

Saddle Stitching

A pamphlet which is made up of a single section can best be bound if saddle stitched. This type of sewing also allows the small book to open flat. The endsheets may be cut as shown in Process 6.

Process 3. Cutting and Applying Endsheets to Books Which Do Not Need Resewing

Materials and Equipment

Endsheet paper
Glue
Board shears, straightedge, knife or shears
Glue brush, glue pot or double boiler

This procedure is for books which do not have to be resewed. It is recommended over the "sewing-on-the-endsheets" method for strength and ease in performing this operation.

Cutting the Endsheets

Two double endsheets are to be cut the length of the book and two times the width of the book. Be sure the the "grain" or easy way of the fold runs lengthwise of the book.

Fold the two double endsheets in the middle, so they will equal the size of the book. If the endsheet has a finished or colored side, be sure to fold this side on the inside.

Applying the Double Endsheet

Glue the two endsheets ¼″ along the folded edges. Place one endsheet (glued side down) on the book so the folded edge comes flush or even with the back edge of the book. Rub the endsheet over its glued portion to insure that it sticks firmly to the book. If the book still has some "backing" on the edge, rub the endsheet down into the joint. Turn the book over and apply the other endsheet in the same manner.

Applying the Backing Flannel

This method of binding does not have a joint strip showing in the endsheet make-up. In order to supply strength in the joint it is necessary to cut the backing flannel 3″ wide plus the width of the back of the book. Be sure that all old glue has been cleaned from the book before applying the flannel. Glue the back edge of the book only and apply the backing flannel so that it extends over onto the front and back endsheets 1½″. Apply a heavy coat of glue on the back edge of the book before applying the flannel. Do not glue the flannel which extends over on the endsheets.

This book is now ready to have its edges finished as shown in Process 13.

Process 4. Cutting and Making Up Endsheets for Books to be Side Sewed (Except Loom Sewing)

Materials and Equipment

Endsheet paper
Joint strips
Glue
Board shears, straightedge, knife, or shears

Glue brush, glue pot or double boiler

Two methods of cutting and making up endsheets are presented, (a) that of using endsheets with the joint strips showing; and (b) a method where the joint strips do not show.

Endsheets Showing Joint Strips

After the books have been separated into sections (provided the book has to be resewed), the next step is to cut the endsheets. The endsheet paper should always be cut so the "grain" or the easy way of the fold of the paper runs lengthwise of the book.

If the book is to be sewed by the overcast method, flat stitched, nailed, or if the endsheets are to be sewed on a book whose original sewing is still good, follow this procedure:

Cut four endsheets exactly the same size as the page of the book. Cut two pieces of joint-strip material 2″ wide and the same length as the book. Protect the top endsheet with a tipping strip and glue, or tip, the four endsheets on the long edge ¼″ (Figure 55) and lay them out on the desk or workbench. Place a piece of the joint strip on the glued surface of the endsheet

Fig. 55. Gluing or Tipping Several Endsheets

so that it projects out beyond the endsheet about 1⅝″. Be sure to put the finished or slick side of the joint strip down or toward the glue. Next, turn this one endsheet and joint strip over and lay the second endsheet flush with the edge and over the joint strip and first endsheet. This will allow one endsheet to extend out over the edge of the other about 1⅝″, Figure 56. Proceed with the second set in the same order.

Glue or "tip" the endsheets ¼″ and fasten to the book with the joint strip up, being sure to have them flush with the back and top of the book. Do not be distrubed by the projection of the one endsheet. Do not cut this projection off.

If this book is to be sewed, the next step is to punch it for stitching or to punch through the endsheets if it does not need to be resewed. See Process 7; if the book is to be nailed, see Process 10.

Endsheets Without Joint Strips Showing

This type of endsheet construction is very popular where the workman does not want the joint strip to show when the book is opened.

Cut a piece of white buckram or special white drill cloth 2″ wide and the length of the book. Glue the strips ¼″ and apply them to the book with the glued side down so that the glued edge of the joint strip comes flush or even with the back edge of the book.

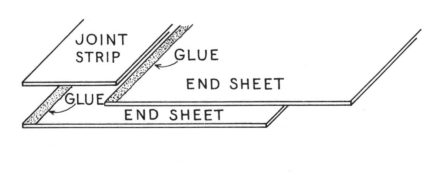

Fig. 56. Making Up Endsheets Using Joint Strips

The book should now be punched for sewing as described in Process 7. The endsheets will be applied after the book has been sewed (Process 10) and the joint strips have been turned back (Process 11).

Process 5. Cutting and Making Up Endsheets for a Loom Sewed Book

Materials and Equipment

Endsheet paper
Joint strips
Glue
Board shears, straightedge, knife or shears
Glue brush, glue pot or double boiler

If the book is to be loom sewed, two methods of making up endsheets are presented in their order of relative strength.

Endsheets with Built-In Joint Strips

The endsheets, like those of an overcast-stitched book, are always the exact length of the book. Cut four endsheets—two ½″ wider than the book, and two 1″ narrower than the width of the book. Cut two pieces of joint strips the exact length of the book and 2″ wide.

Glue or "tip" the four endsheets about ¼″ and lay them on the desk. Place a piece of joint strip on the glued surface of the narrower endsheets so that it projects out beyond the endsheet about 1⅝″ (place the slick or finished side of the joint strip toward the glue). Next, turn this over and lay the second endsheet to extend out over the edge of the other about ¼″.

These endsheets are not fastened to the book until the book has been sawed out (Process 8). Lay the endsheets on the table with the joint strip down and away from you; turn up and fold this edge (where the joint strip and endsheet are glued) toward you. Fold over about ⅜″ and crease with a bone folder. For the next step turn to Process 8.

Endsheets with Joint Strips Not Showing

If the workman does not want the joint strip to show when the book is opened, cut two pieces of special white drill cloth or white buckram 2" wide and the length of the book. The joint strips will not be applied until the book has been sawed out, Process 8.

Process 6. Cutting and Making Up Endsheets for Saddle Stitched Books

Materials and Equipment

Endsheet paper
Joint strips
Glue
Board shears, straightedge, or shears
Glue brush
Glue pot or double boiler

Books that are to be saddle stitched are usually pamphlets or groups of pages folded into a single section. Saddle stitching is never used except where there is only one section to the complete book.

Cut one endsheet the length of the pamphlet or book and twice the width plus ½". Cut two more endsheets the same size as the book. Cut one piece of joint strip 2" wide and the length of the book. The endsheets are now ready to be made up.

Making Up the Endsheet with the Joint Strip Showing

Fold the large endsheet over and crease it in the middle of the sheet so that it is about the same size as the book. Glue or tip the two small endsheets on their long edge and unfinished side about ¼" and lay them on the table with the glued edges up. Holding the joint strip with the finished side down, cover the one glued edge of one endsheet, leaving about 1¾" of the joint strip extending out from the endsheet; place the other edge of the joint strip over the glued edge of the second endsheet. This fastens the two endsheets to the finished side of the joint strip and leaves about 1½" of its finished side showing between them. Make a crease lengthwise of the joint strip and fold it over so that the finished side is in the inside of the fold. This fold should run down the exact middle of the joint strip. The endsheets are now ready to be applied to the pamphlet.

Making Up the Endsheet with the Joint Strip Not Showing

If the workman desires a type of binding on which the joint strip does not show, cut two endsheets the length of the pamphlet or book and twice the width plus ½". Cut a piece of special white drill cloth or a piece of sign cloth 2" wide.

Fold the two endsheets over, creasing them in the middle of the sheet so they are about the same size as the book. Open one of the endsheets and lay it on the table with the fold on the outside.   ·

Glue the joint strip and place it so it is centered over the fold. This endsheet, with the joint strip on the outside, takes the place of the "made-up" endsheet in the previous section (where the joint strip shows).

Applying the Endsheets

Tip or glue the back edge of the pamphlet, which is probably little more than a fold 1/16" in thickness. Place the pamphlet on the inside of the folded double endsheet, so the glued edge of the pamphlet is fastened to the inside of the folded endsheet.

Place (but do not glue) the other "made-up" endsheet so that the crease in the joint strip, or fold in the paper, folds around the double endsheet. The pamphlet is now ready to be punched and sewed as shown in Process 9.

Chapter 7

Punching and Sewing

Process 7. Punching Book for Side Sewing (Except Loom Sewing)

Equipment
Stabber or equivalent
Diamond pointed awl

Procedure
Whether or not your book is to be overcast, machine stitched, or flat stitched, the procedure is the same in punching the book. If the book is ¾" or less in thickness, it is generally flat stitched or machine stitched. Machine stitching is preferred. If it is thicker than ¾", it is overcast.

If a stabber is available, place the book with the back edge against the back gauge of the stabber or the punching board so it will be centered under the series of needles. Feed the book in such a manner that the top edge will be against the adjustable gauge and the back against the rear gauge of the stabber. In this way punch the entire book, taking two to three sections at a time. Avoid trying to punch too many sections at one time.

If hand equipment is being used, the book must be fed to the punching gauge section by section and punched by hand with the awl or series of awls. Place the top edge of each section of the book against the adjustable gauge and the back or folded edge of the book against the long gauge.

A hand drill may be used to drill small holes for sewing.

Punching for Sewing on Endsheets

If the sewing of the book is in good condition (Process 2), and the endsheets or the joint strips have been glued on the book, use a small awl to punch a series of holes along the back edge as described in the next paragraph.

Mark a pencil line along the back edge of the joint strip about ¼" from the edge. Mark lines 1" from the top and bottom of the book: punch holes about 1" apart on the line along the back edge holding the awl at an angle so that it comes out two or three sections below. This method is *not recommended* for general practice.

Process 8. Sawing Out the Book for Loom Sewing

Equipment

Finishers clamp
Fourteen-point or fifteen-point backsaw
V trough

A loom-sewed book has an advantage over other types of sewing in that it will lie flat when open. It is not as strong a sewing as other types, but is very desirable for music books, Bibles, and other similar volumes. A book must be made up of a series of sections to be loom sewed. Magazines may be also sewed by this method if they are made up of complete sections.

Procedure

Before the made-up endsheets or joint strips can be put on a loom-sewed book, it is necessary that the book be sawed out. Sawing out is accomplished by putting the book, with pieces of binders board on each side, between a finishers clamp or the backer so the back edge of the book extends about ½" above the clamp. Be sure the book is held firmly.

Mark lines across the back edge of the book—1″ from the top and bottom edges. This line is where the kettle cord or soft twine is to go. Using a fine-toothed backsaw, cut a groove so that a piece of kettle cord will just fit into it (slightly less than ⅛″ deep). This can be accomplished by tilting the saw from one side to the other so as to make the groove wider than the saw. Saw to the depth of the middle sheet of each section.

Next, measure between the saw cuts for the tapes, which are always equidistant between the cords. The tapes should be from 2″ to 3″ apart—the number depends on the length of the book. A 10″ or 12″ book would not have more than three tapes. Draw lines at right angles to the edge of the book through these outside points to help guide in sawing. Saw on these marks to the depth of half the thickness of the heaviest section in the book, which means sawing through the fold to the middle sheet of each section. Some binders still prefer to work entirely with cords in place of the cord-and-tape combination described here. If cords alone are used, make a single saw cut for each one.

To lend strength to the sewing, cut two strips of gummed tape or vellum, ½″ wide and the length of the book. Open the first and last sections of the book at the exact center. Moisten the tape and place over the fold in each of the two sections as shown in Figure 57. Use an awl to punch through the tape at points previously sawed in the sections.

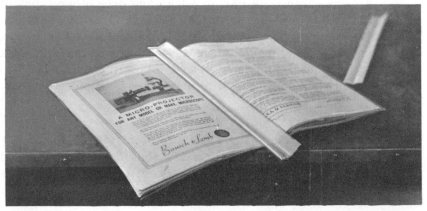

Fig. 57. In Loom Sewing, Apply Gummed Tape to the First and Last Sections

Applying the Built-In-Joint Type of Endsheet

Take the front and back sections from the book and tip the front of the back section and back of the front section $\frac{3}{8}''$. Lay the folded edge of the endsheets on the glued edges (with the folded edge toward the inside of the book), and let them dry, so that when the edges are folded around the sections the joint strips will be on the outside of the book. Place the front and back sections one at a time in the V trough and use the awl to punch holes through the previously sawed-out places, going through the joint strip and endsheets on both sections. The loom or sewing frame should be set up, and sewing may be started on the book, Process 11.

Applying Endsheets Where Joint Strips Do Not Show

After the book has been sawed out, and if the workman desires endsheets which do not allow the joint strips to show, the following procedure should be followed:

Take the two pieces of joint strips which have been previously cut (Process 5) and glue each $\frac{3}{8}''$ along one edge. Place one joint strip on the back of the front section so it extends out of the back edge of the book $1\frac{5}{8}''$. Place the other joint strip on the front of the back section so it extends out of the back edge of the book $1\frac{5}{8}''$.

After the glue has dried for a few minutes, fold the two joint strips around the sections to which they were just fastened so that the extensions are on the outside of the front and back sections respectively.

Holes should now be punched from the inside through sawed places into the joint strip. This should be done in a V trough with the use of an awl. Next apply a $\frac{1}{2}''$ strip of gummed tape down the middle of the front and back sections on the inside of the fold. Using an awl, punch holes through the tape at the sawed places. The book is now ready to be sewed (Process 11).

After the book has been sewed, cut two endsheets the length of the book and twice the width. The endsheets should be cut so that the grain or "easy" way of the fold runs parallel to the length of the book. Fold the double endsheets lengthwise so they are about the same size as the book. Glue the folded edges ¼″ and place them flush with the back edge of the book and under the joint strips. Holding the book so it rests on the back edge, glue the portion of the joint strip which extends out from the book, and then press it against the endsheets. Rub and be sure it is fastened securely. The workman is now ready to fray the ends of the cords and glue the "slips" as outlined in Process 11.

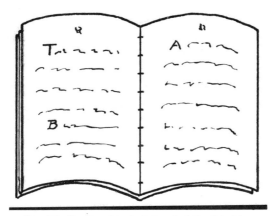

Fig. 58. Section Marked for Saddle Stitching

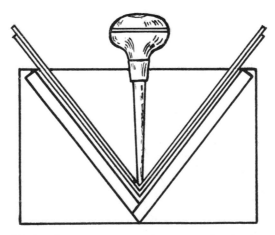

Fig. 59. Punching Sections in V Trough for Saddle Stitching

Process 9. Punching Book for Saddle Stitching

Equipment

Scratch awl

V trough for punching

Procedure

Open the pamphlet to the middle of all the folded pages. This is where the turned ends of the wire staples will be found if the pamphlet has been previously stapled. Mark lines ½″ from the top and bottom edges of the book. Divide the remaining distance so that the marks will be from ⅝″ to 1″ apart, Figure 58.

Place the book in the V trough (Figure 59) and punch straight through each of the marks which have just been made, Figure 58. The book is now ready to be sewed (Process 12).

Process 10. Side Sewing (Except Loom Sewing)

Materials and Equipment

Linen thread

Sewing bench or loom

Needle

There are many methods of sewing books, seven of which appear in this book. Each serves a specific purpose and must be used as determined by the needs and type of book to be bound.

Sewing on the Endsheets

Sewing on the endsheets of a book is one of the simplest types of sewing, but is *not recommended for average library binding*. For this method, No. 16 linen thread is recommended. After the needle has been threaded, start sewing with a downward motion through the endsheet and the sections through which the holes were punched. Tie the thread in the end hole of one endsheet which was punched with the awl. Sew over and over until the other side of the book is reached. Go into the end hole twice and return to the other edge. This will make a crossstitch. Turn the book over and repeat the process on the other endsheet, Figure 60. The endsheets are now ready to be turned back as shown in Process 13. As was previously indicated this method is *not* recommended for general practice.

Flat Stitching

Each section of the book should have previously been punched. Always use No. 12 thread in flat stitching. Thread the needle and make a tie through the end hole, going through all of the sections, or entire book. Be sure always to push the needle downward and in the direction in which the holes were punched, come out over the back, and down the next hole. Sew from one side to the other and return to the starting point. Make a tie and turn back the endsheets as shown in Process 13.

Notice that this sewing makes a cross-stitch, Figure 61. Avoid sewing a book by flat stitching if it is more than $\frac{3}{4}''$ thick. Books more than $\frac{3}{4}''$ thick should be sewed by the overcast method.

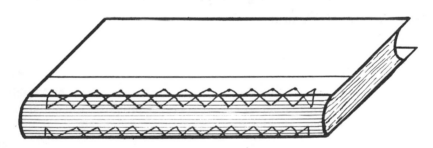

Fig. 60. Appearance of Sewed-On Endsheets

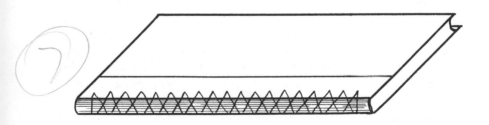

Fig. 61. Appearance of a Flat-Stitched Book

Machine Stitching

The term "machine stitching" is used for lack of a better name. It is sometimes called the up-and-down kind of sewing. It is a type of sewing which would be produced by a sewing machine if it were run along the back edge of the book. This type of sewing is a form of flat stitching, but it is superior to regular flat stitching. A difficulty arises in bringing the threads back up through every other hole against the direction the hole was punched. This can be overcome if the holes are drilled or perforated.

Start the sewing by going down through the end hole (Figure 62) and then up through the next until the book is crossed. Start back, and end the sewing by tying the two ends as shown in Figure 63. The endsheets are now ready to be turned back as shown in Process 13.

Overcast Sewing

The overcast method of sewing is one of the strongest types. The book on which it is used will not open as flat as books on which other types of sewing have been used, but this method

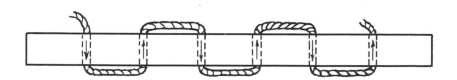

Fig. 62. Beginning of Machine Stitching

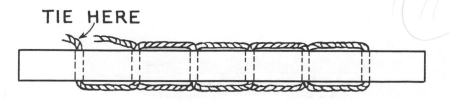

TIE HERE

Fig. 63. Completed Machine Stitching

is a strong way of fastening sections together. The size of the thread used in overcast sewing is generally determined by the thickness of and number of sections in the book. If there are many small sections, a light thread, No. 20, is best; but if the sections are large and few in number, use No. 16 thread. On the book of average size, fiction and the like, use No. 16.

The workman using this method sews one or two and sometimes three sections at a time. The thickness of the sections will determine the number. A combined total thickness not to exceed 5/16″ is best. Take the front section or group of sections, tie in the end hole, and sew over and over to the other edge of the book, using a downward stroke and sewing in the direction the holes are punched, Figure 64. Add another section or group of sections and sew through both groups together using the same stitch, Figure 65. When the third section or group of sections

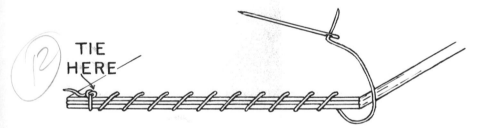

Fig. 64. Sewing First Group of Sections in Overcast Sewing

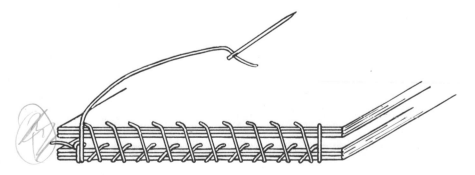

Fig. 65. Sewing Second Group of Sections in Overcast Sewing

is added, the needle must come out between the first and second group of sections. In this manner the book is held by sewing two groups of sections together at a time, Figure 66. The last group is sewed twice so that it makes a cross-stitch on the joint strip of the endsheets. The endsheets must now be turned back as shown in Process 13.

Process 11. Loom Sewing

Materials and Equipment

    Linen thread
    Kettle cord
    Tape
    Sewing bench or loom
    Needle

Procedure

    After the book has been sawed out, the endsheets glued on or stay cloth applied, and the holes punched through the joint strip, set up the loom or sewing frame in the following manner:

    Cut two pieces of kettle cord or heavy soft twine and the number of tapes necessary, each 1 yard in length. Linen tape is preferred to cotton. Place the book near the center of the loom

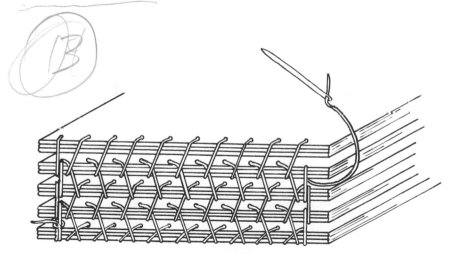

Fig. 66. Appearance of Completed Overcast Sewing

and adjust the tapes and cord to the sawed places on the back edge of the book by using nails to fasten the tapes and cords at the bottom of the loom. Tie the cords or tape at the top, Figure 67.

If the book is of average size and has heavy sections, use No. 12 thread. If the book has many small sections, use No. 20 or smaller. Again the number and thickness of the sections determines the size of the thread to be used. To illustrate: If you are binding a large single section magazine such as *Life*, twelve issues to the volume, use No. 12 thread. If, however, you are binding a magazine such as the *National Geographic*, which has many sections to each issue, six issues to the volume, No. 30 thread should be used. Reducing the size of the thread reduces the amount of the swell in the book. A large dictionary or Bible would be sewed with No. 30 or No. 35 thread, using the "two-on" method, Figure 68.

Select the thread and start sewing by tying a slip knot around the kettle cord at one side or the other and even with the base of the loom. Place either the top or bottom section of the book on the loom so that the endsheet will be down, and then draw the thread into the end hole (**A**, Figure 67) made for the kettle cord. Be sure the needle comes out in the center of the section. Bring the thread out the next hole (**B**, Figure 67) around the tape or cord and back through the center of the section (**C**, Figure 67). Repeat this until you come out the other end hole (**F**, Figure 67) at the kettle cord. Tie a knot to hold your sewing around the kettle cord. Place another section on the first,

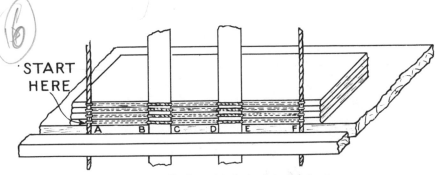

Fig. 67. All-Along Method of Loom Sewing

making sure that the paging is correct. Proceed in the same manner as above, remembering to come out around the tapes or cords and tying to the kettle cord whenever the thread reaches the end hole. This procedure is called the "all-along" method.

On thick books with many sections, it is sometimes necessary to sew the book in such a manner as to reduce the amount of "swell." This can be done by sewing the book by the "two-on" method as shown in Figure 68. This is ordinarily used on thick Bibles, dictionaries, or magazines. The loom is set up, using kettle cords and tapes (or all cords) in the same manner as for "all-along" loom sewing. Sew three or four sections of the book, using the all-along method. Place two sections above these and draw the thread into the end hole made for the kettle cord (Figure 68, G). Be sure the needle comes out in the center of the section. Bring the thread out the next hole, H, around the tape or cord and back through I, which is in the next section. Come out from the center of this section at hole F, then go around the tape or cord and into hole K in the lower section or into the section where the sewing was just started with the two-on method. Bring the thread out of hole L and tie a knot on the kettle cord. Place two more sections on the book and

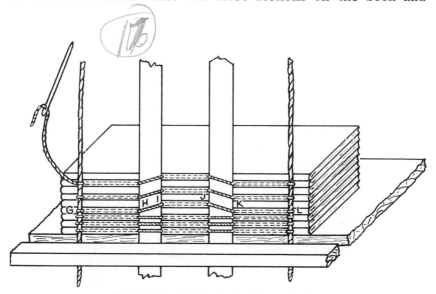

Fig. 68. Two-On Method of Loom Sewing

proceed in the same manner as in the last two sections as shown in Figure 67. The all-along method is then used on the last three or four sections of the book.

The workman will notice that with the same amount of thread one can sew two sections to the book by the "two-on" method where only one section may be sewed by the "all-along" method. The two-on is not as substantial a sewing method, but it is necessary to use it when a large book has many small sections.

After the workman has finished sewing, the tapes and cords are cut so as to allow at least 1″ on each side of the book. These extensions of the tapes and cords are called "slips."

After the book has been sewed, the first and last sections should be glued ¼″ to the sections next to them. This is done by opening the book between these sections and applying the necessary glue with a small brush.

If the book is to have endsheets where the joint strips do not show, the endsheets should now be applied as shown in Process 8. Otherwise, proceed as follows:

Fray the ends of the cords on both sides of the book. Glue the "slips" (the cords and tapes) on one side of the book and fasten them to the joint strip and allow to dry. After they are dry, turn the book over and use the backing or cobbler's hammer to pound the sections so as to press out any fullness or

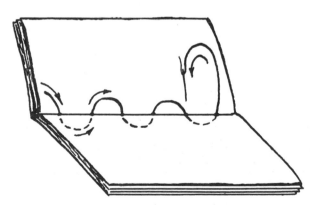

Fig. 69. Saddle Stitching First Direction

"swell." Glue the slips on this side of the book, stretch the cords and tapes, and fasten them down to the joint strip. Keep a weight on these until they are dry. The book is now ready to have the reinforcement material applied to the back edge, Process 14.

Process 12. Saddle Stitching and Nailing

Materials and Equipment

Linen thread
Nails
Hammer

Procedure for Saddle Sewing

Saddle stitching is accomplished in the same manner as machine stitching, except that the pamphlet is opened and sewed "through the fold" as shown in Figure 69. Figure 70 shows the book after the sewing has been completed. If the pamphlet is of heavy paper, it is advisable to put a piece of gummed tape down the fold on the inside and punch it before sewing, as was recommended for the first and last sections of loom-sewed books.

Generally a saddle-stitched book is not rounded or backed, but a piece of flannel is applied to put a swell in the back and to hold the sewing in place. Process 14 lists the directions for applying the flannel.

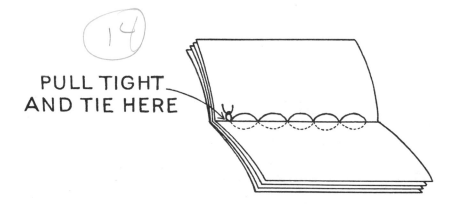

PULL TIGHT
AND TIE HERE

Fig. 70. Completed Saddle Stitching

Procedure for Nailing

If the book to be nailed is made up of single sheets, the back edges of the pages should first be "jogged." Jogging is making the pages come flush to the back and top by alternately lifting and dropping the edges of the pages on a table or pounding iron until they are even. The pages should then be glued lightly on the back of the book and allowed to dry. The endsheets should next be tipped on to the book and marked for nailing. Draw a line along the joint strip, 1/4" from the back edge. Make two marks—one 3/4" from the top or bottom and another 1 1/4" from the other, Figure 71. Divide the space between the two marks into distances of about 3/4" to 1", Figure 71. The book is now ready to be nailed on one side.

Place the book in a clamp with the back edge out so as to hold it in position while nailing. Use nails which are about three-fourths the thickness of the book; generally shingle, lath, or box nails are satisfactory. Always use nails with large flat heads. Bindery supply houses have special nails that interlock. Drive them into the book as shown in Figure 71 about 1/4" to 3/8" from the back edge of the book, depending on the width of the margins, size of the book, and size of the nails. Turn the book over and drive nails in on the other side and repeat the above process, being sure to stagger the nails as shown in Figure 71.

After all the nails have been driven in place, cut two pieces of endsheet paper 3/8" wide and the length of the book,

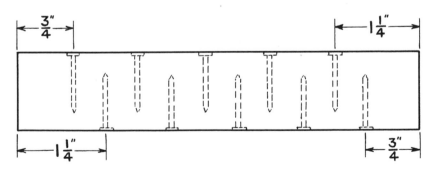

Fig. 71. Nailing Layout

and glue them over the heads of the nails. This is done to keep them from rusting through the joint strip.

The book is now ready to have its endsheets turned back (Process 13). NOTE: Do not attempt to round a book which has been nailed, as this is impossible; however, it may be backed slightly after the trimming process. As was previously stated, nailing is an expeditious method and is not recommended for general practice.

Process 13. Handling the Endsheets After Sewing

Turning Back the Endsheets or Joint Strips

After the sewing has been completed, either by machine stitching, nailing, flat stitching, overcast sewing, or where the endsheets have been sewed on, it is necessary to turn back the endsheets. Using the bone folder, turn back the joint strip away from the book and even with the sewing, not more than ⅜" from the back edge. Next, fold the joint strip back toward the book, making the fold flush with the back edge. Glue this small space, which covers the sewing, and rub the folded joint strip with the bone folder until it sticks. Put a brick on the book while the glue dries. The process allows the joint to open at the edge of the book and makes it more difficult for the covers to be torn off.

Turning Back Endsheets and Covering Joint Strips

Two double endsheets are cut the length of the book and twice its width. Be sure that the "grain" or easy way of the fold runs lengthwise of the book.

Fold the two double endsheets in the middle, so they will equal the size of the book. If the endsheet has a finished or colored side, be sure to fold it on the inside.

After the joint strips have been folded back, the two previously cut endsheets are glued ¼" along one side of the folded edge. The endsheets are applied on the ⅜" fold of the joint strip over the sewing, leaving 1¼" of the joint strip without glue. Place the book with its back edge on a piece of waste paper and flatten down the two 1¼" pieces of the joint strip. Pull them up over the endsheets and rub well. Place a weight on the book so the joint strips on the endsheets will dry flat.

Checking Paging

The next step is to check the paging of the book carefully. This is done by quickly scanning page numbers to be sure they run consecutively. If a section is found to be upside down or in the wrong place, the book will have to be completely torn down and resewed to correct the error. After the paging has been checked, the book is ready to have the flannel or other reinforcement material applied on the back edge as shown in Process 14.

Chapter 8

Forwarding

Process 14. Applying Backing Flannel or Other Reinforcement Material

Materials

Flannel or equivalent

Procedure

The reinforcement material on the back of a book may be a good grade of flannel which can be obtained at any dry-goods store. Occasionally unbleached muslin is used, but it is not as satisfactory as the flannel. This material should be cut ½″ shorter than the book and ¾″ wider than the thickness of the back edge of the book. The back edge of the book must be glued heavily because the flannel will absorb most of the glue. Glue from the center of the back edge toward the ends; never from the ends to the center. If regular backing flannel is used, the "fuzzy" or "furry" side should be applied toward the glue. The flannel should be rubbed well after it has been applied to the newly glued back and should lap over the side edges about ⅜″.

The book is now ready to have its edges finished, Process 15.

Process 15. Finishing the Edges of Books

Equipment

Cutting machine
Belt or disk sander
Plough and cutting press
Beveled chisel

Using the Cutting Machine

After the paging has been checked and the flannel applied, the book is ready to be trimmed. First, place the book approximately in the middle of the cutting machine with its back edge against the back gauge and with the front edge toward the workman. Run the gauge forward so as to take a trim of about ⅛″ or less from the front edge of the book. Place a piece of binders board on the book. Hold the book with the left hand so the back edge stays tight against the back gauge; then tighten the clamp with the right hand. Place both hands on the handle which controls the blade, release the lock, and make the cut.

Loosen the clamp and turn the book so that the top edge is against the back gauge and the back edge is against the left side of the cutting machine if the knife cuts from right to left. Adjust back gauge so as to trim about ⅛″ from the bottom or "tail" edge. Place the binders board over the book, tighten the clamp, and cut as before. Be sure to hold the back edge of the book against the left side of the machine while the clamp is being tightened. Release the clamp.

Trim the top by putting the bottom edge of the book against the back gauge and the back edge against the left side of the cutting machine. Be sure that the clamp is down tight before making a cut. If the knife of the machine you are using cuts from left to right, work on the right side in place of the left as directed above.

Sanding the Edges

Sanding the edges of a book is a method which is not as satisfactory as trimming with a cutting machine, although it does have a value for cleaning purposes.

Place two pieces of scrap binders board flush with the edge of the book which is to be sanded and put the book in the finisher's clamp so that this edge extends out about ½".

If a belt sander is being used, a table which is perpendicular to the belt may be constructed. Hold the edge of the book against the sanding belt until it is clean. Using the above procedure, finish the other two edges.

If a disk sander is used, the above procedure may be followed. If a lathe is used, a block may be placed on the bed for a guide in feeding the book squarely into the sanding disk. (See Figure 20.)

Using the Beveled Chisel

A satisfactory job of finishing the edges of the book can be accomplished by using a heavy chisel, ¾" or 1" in width and beveled to an angle of 30°.

Drawing guidelines for using this method is called "marking-up." Draw a line on the front endsheet ⅛" in from the front edge. Draw a line on the front endsheet about ⅛" in from the top edge. Repeat on the back endsheet at the bottom edge.

Cut two pieces of binders board larger than the book. Glue front endsheet in three or four spots and place one of the boards so it is flush with the lines drawn on the front and top edges of the book and extends over the bottom. Place the other board on the back endsheet in the same manner, making sure that it is flush with the line drawn on the bottom edge and extends over the other two edges.

Place the book on the special finishing or cutting press so that the front endsheet is to the left of the workman and the board placed on the front endsheet is flush with the top of the press. The press should be placed in front of the workman so that the chisel will cut from the left side of the book. Tighten the press so that the book is held securely.

Hold the handle of the chisel with the left hand and the chisel itself with the right so that it will lie flat on the wide edge of the clamp or press. (See Figure 21.) Push the chisel forward along the book, cutting about ⅛" at a time with the chisel point. Cut only on the forward strokes.

The front edge of the book should be trimmed first, so that, if the edge "breaks out" at the corner, it may be cut off when the top and bottom edges are cut.

After finishing the front edge, place the book in the press with the top edge up and the back edge away from the workman, being sure the board on the endsheet comes flush with the top of the clamp or press. Cut as before. If the book is of soft paper and the edge has a tendency to break out, it will be seen that this break will occur at the back edge. This can be filled and covered when the headbands are applied. After this edge is cut, remove the book from the press, turn it around and over, and place it in the press so that the back edge is away from the workman and the cutting board is flush with the press. Proceed as before. The chisel must be kept sharp.

Using the Plough and Cutting Press

The plough and cutting press method is a carryover from the earliest method of finishing edges of books. It is not "foolproof," and much care should be taken in its use.

"Mark up" as in the preceding section. Draw a line on the front endsheet $\frac{1}{8}''$ in from the front edge. Draw a line on the front endsheet about $\frac{1}{8}''$ in from the bottom edge. Repeat on the back endsheet at the top edge.

Cut two pieces of binders board larger than the book. Glue the front endsheet in three or four spots; place one of the boards so it is flush with the lines drawn on the front and bottom edges. Place the other board on the back endsheet in the same manner except that it must be flush with the line drawn on the top edge and extend over the other two edges.

Place the book in the cutting press so the front endsheet will come to the right of the workman. The board placed on the front endsheet should be flush with the top of the press. The press should be placed in front of the workman so that the knife will cut from the right side of the book. Tighten the press and place the plough in position.

Feed the knife so that it touches the front endsheets, and push the plough forward. Cut only on forward strokes, and tighten the knife each time before starting a forward stroke. A more satisfactory job may be done if a slight cut is made each time. The front edge of the book should be trimmed first, so that if the edge "breaks out" at the corner it may be cut off when the top edge is cut.

After finishing the front edge, place the book in press with the bottom edge up and the back edge away from the workman, making sure the board on the endsheet comes flush with the top of the press. Cut as before. After this edge is cut, take the book out of the press, turn it around and over, and place it in the press so the back edge is away from the workman and the cutting board is flush with the press. Proceed as before.

Making Round Corners

If round corners are desired, they may be sanded, cut with a gouge, or rounded on a round cornering machine. If sandpaper or a gouge is used, the book must be held firmly in a finisher's clamp. The gouge must be sharp and care must be exercised in its use to keep from cutting into the straight edges of the book.

Process 16. Rounding and Backing

Equipment

Backing hammer

Backer or backing boards

After the book is trimmed, it is ready to be rounded and backed. If the flannel was glued the day preceding this backing operation, dampen it slightly with a sponge.

Rounding the Book

The back of the book is rounded with a backing or cobbler's hammer. Place the front edge toward you, holding the book with the left hand so the fingers are on top and the thumb is in the center of the front edge. Push the middle section away from the thumb and draw the top edge toward you with the fingers as they rest on it. Hit along the back edge with the backing hammer; and if the book is properly held, it should form a "round," Figure 72. Turn the book over and repeat the above procedure. Books that are stubborn in taking a round may need to be hammered from both sides several times. Do not attempt to round a book which has been flat stitched, machine stitched, saddle stitched, or nailed.

Fig. 72. Rounding the Book

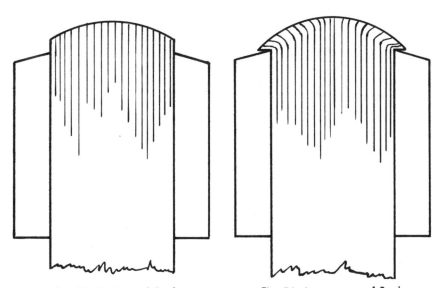

Fig. 73. Position of Book
in Backer

Fig. 74. Appearance of Book
After Being Backed

Backing the Book

After the book is rounded, it is put in the backer or between backing boards with its back edge up. On average books allow the back edge to extend above the backer from 3/16" to ¼", Figure 73. This measurement varies because of the different thicknesses of binding boards to be used and the size of the book itself. Larger books must have heavier boards than thin or small books; consequently, the back edge must be farther above the backer in order to produce a sufficient "joint." By using the backing hammer and hitting a glancing blow from the center of the back toward each side, the edge that extends above the backer is turned out, Figure 74. Care should be taken not to hit this edge too hard, as the joint strip and outer edge may be cut. Backing is not always necessary in the binding of a book, but it gives a better appearance and allows a joint to be made between the cover and the back. Figure 74 shows the book in the backer after it has been backed. Pounding is usually done first on the outer third of each side of the back edge, Figure 75. The last blows should be directed toward the center of the back edge to set the round. An experienced craftsman may vary this procedure.

Headbands should now be applied, Process 17.

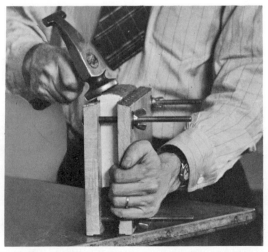

Fig. 75. Backing the Book in the Combination Backer and Press

Process 17. Applying the Headbands

Material

Headband material

Headbands are ornamental pieces made either from cotton or silk and are applied on most bindings. A method for making them is described in Chapter 4, p. 54.

Procedure

After the book has been rounded and backed, two pieces of headband material are cut the width of the back edge of the book. The top and bottom edges of the back are tipped about ½″, and it is best to glue this space with the tip of the finger, which will tend to prevent glue running over the edges. The colored or finished edges of the bands face in toward the front edge of the book, Figure 76. Care should be taken not to let the bands extend into the joints—cut them the exact width of the back edge.

Headbands do not add any strength or serve any purpose other than to make the book more attractive.

After the headbands have been put on, the spring back is applied, Process 18.

Process 18. Making the Spring Back

Material

Spring-back paper or lightweight wrapping paper

Fig. 76. Applying the Headbands

Two methods of cutting and applying spring backs are presented here. While both are good, the first is preferred in that it permits the entire back to break away from the book and it is sometimes easier to apply. The purpose of the spring back, sometimes called "hollow back," is to fasten the back edge of the book directly to the cover and yet allow the book to "break away" from the cover.

Three-Times-the-Width-of-the-Back Method

Cut a piece of spring-back paper exactly three times the width of the back edge of the book and 1″ longer than the book. Make sure that the easy way of the fold (grain) runs lengthwise with the book.

Fold this piece in exact thirds, the exact size of the width of the back of the book, and glue one-third of the spring back as shown in Figure 77. Glue the back side of A, Figure 77, only. Fold the paper, Figure 78, A, so that the glued portion comes on the inside, Figure 78, B, and press the other third down over it, Figure 78, C. Dampen both sides of the spring back with a

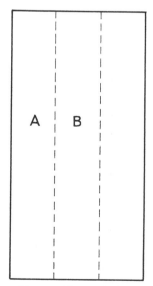

Fig. 77. Three-Times-
the-Width Spring Back

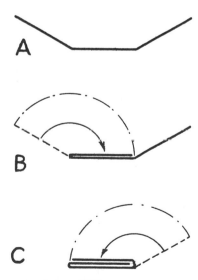

Fig. 78. Gluing the Three-Times-
the-Width Spring Back

sponge. Glue the entire back edge of the book and place the spring back on it so that the single thickness of the paper, **B**, Figure 78, is fastened directly to the book and the two thicknesses of the spring back come to the outside. Rub the spring back so that it sticks at all points along the flannel.

After the spring back is dry, the extension at the top and bottom edges may be trimmed next to the headbands.

If the book is an extremely large one, cut the spring-back paper four times the width of the back of the book and 1" longer, and fold in exact fourths as shown in Figure 79. Cut a piece of super cloth or muslin exactly three times the width of the back of the book. Glue the back edge of the book and place the muslin or super cloth so that one-third extends on each side of the book (dotted lines, Figure 80, **A**). Dampen the spring back and lightly glue that portion of the super cloth which is over the back edge, and place the **C** part, Figure 79, over the glued portion of the book, Figure 80, **A**. Fold part **D**, Figure 80, **B**, over into **C** and glue the top of **D**. Fold the muslin or super cloth over into the

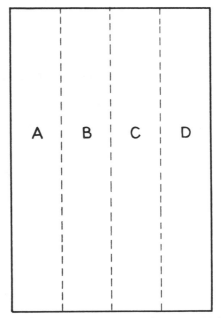

Fig. 79. Four-Times-the-Width Spring Back

glued portion, Figure 80, **C**, and reglue and fold **B** onto this material, Figure 80, **D**. Next glue the top of **B** and draw in the extending muslin or super cloth, Figure 80, **E**. Reglue the muslin and draw **A** over onto this material as shown in Figure 80, **F**. Rub the spring back well with a bone folder. After it is dry, the extension at the top and bottom edges may be trimmed off next to the headbands. This method is stronger than the one in the preceding paragraphs.

Three-and-One-Half-Times Method

Cut a piece of spring-back paper $3\frac{1}{2}$ times the width of the back edge of the book and 1″ longer than the book. Again the grain should run lengthwise with the book.

Dampen one side of the spring-back paper with a sponge and glue the flannel heavily. The paper, dry side against the glue, is put across the back of the book, leaving a glued space of about 3/16″ showing along one edge. It is then folded at the other edge and pulled back across the entire back, allowing the 3/16″ glued space to hold it in place. Again it must be folded at the edge and glued solid across the back on the inside of the

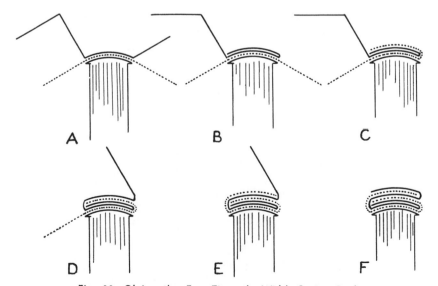

Fig. 80. Gluing the Four-Times-the-Width Spring Back

fold. The first fold leaves an unglued space in the spring back. A good rubbing with the bone folder will insure the paper's sticking. The spring back is the life of the book, as it allows the back of the book to be glued to the back of the cover and yet break away from the cover. This is an advantage over most commercially bound books.

On large books, this type of spring back may also be reinforced. Cut the spring back $4\frac{1}{2}$ times the width of the back of the book, with the easy fold running lengthwise with the book. Cut a piece of super cloth or muslin 3 times the width of the back edge of the book. Glue the back edge of the book and place the muslin over the glued surface so that it is centered with one third extending on each side of the book. Glue the portion of muslin which is directly over the back edge of the book. Dampen the spring back and place it over the glued portion, leaving 3/16" space as in the paragraph above. Make the first fold back over the back of the book and over the small glued space. Rub the spring back and fold again on this edge. Glue the inside of the fold of the spring back and draw in the muslin on one side; reglue and draw the spring back paper over this material. Make a fold on the edge and glue on the inside of the spring back; draw over the piece of muslin. Glue this material and fold over the spring-back paper. Rub the back with the bone folder so that it will stick at all places. After the spring back is dry, crease the remaining paper along the edge and tear it off. Cut off the extending back at the top and bottom edges next to the headbands.

Chapter 9

Making Covers for Full Binding

Process 19. Cutting the Cover Boards

Materials

Binders board

Procedure

In cutting the covers for a book, be accurate in taking all measurements. While both covers will always be the same length, they will usually vary in width because of irregularities which occur in rounding and backing. The *square* (a term which will appear many times) is the distance of the projection of the covers over each of the three edges of the book, and is sometimes equal to the thickness of the board used; or a standard ⅛″ may be accepted. However, when very light board is used for covers, the square should never be less than **D** board, Figure 46, or ⅛″.

The thickness of the board should first be determined. On average books (8- or 9-inch length), **D** board, Figure 46, is satisfactory. If the books are small (6- or 7-inch length) a lighter board should be used (**E**, Figure 46); if they are large, a heavier board (**C**, Figure 46) will be required. Covers for books about 8½ x 11 inches may be cut from C board, Figure 46; and a **B** board, Figure 46, should be used on the very large books.

The board should first be cut the length of the book plus the square at the top and bottom edges. Place one of the boards thus cut on the front of the book with its edge tight against the joint formed in backing. Make a line on the board flush with the front edge of the book. Cut off on this pencil line. Mark the inside of this cover board "F" and the outside of the endsheet "F." Turn the book over and repeat this operation on the back. Mark the inside of the back cover board and the outside of the back endsheet with the letter "B."

If round corners are desired on the book, the outside corners of the cover boards are rounded to conform to the round corners of the book itself. This should be done before the board is glued to the binding material.

Plan the cutting of the boards so as to avoid waste. If the book is not to be backed, allow 1/8″ along the back edge for a space when measuring. In other words, on books that have not been backed, always cut the cover the width of the book less 1/8″. When the covers are pulled out to make a square on the front edge, it forms the space for a joint along the back of the book. Always be sure that the covers are marked on the inside of each with an "F" for the front and a "B" for the back. Be sure that the covers are cut with a square on the top and bottom, and that they are cut flush with the front edge of the book. If the workman is binding more than one book, mark the covers and endsheets "F₁," "F₂," "F₃," *et cetera*, so that covers for books will not become mixed.

NOTE: *Continue with Processes 20 through 27 if you are working with a full binding. For half, three-quarter and quarter bindings, use Processes 28 through 37. Processes up to this point are used with all types of books.*

Process 20. Cutting Binding Materials for Full Bindings

Materials

Coated fabric, vinyl, buckram, leather, bookcloth, gingham, or any suitable binding material
Ragboard or lightweight redboard

Cutting the Covering Material

After the cover boards have been cut to size, binding materials for full bindings should be cut.

First determine the color and kind of binding material desired. Sometimes this is specified by the owner. If there are no scraps big enough to use, cut a strip—across the width of the roll or from yard pieces—1½″ longer than the covers or 2″ longer than the book. The general practice is to cut across the entire width of the roll as the remnant can always be used.

Place the book on the binding material with a 1″ margin on the front edge; pull the material around and over the other cover and measure 1″ beyond the second cover for turn-in. Cut the material off and put what is not going to be used back into the roll.

If leather is to be used, a paper pattern should first be prepared, according to the above procedure. It is then transferred to a skin of leather by powdering around the pattern. This method will save material.

NOTE: If the lettering is to be done with an electric pen, a material with a smooth surface should be selected. This type of lettering is difficult to apply on a rough surface.

Cutting the Lettering Strip

Cut a scrap of endsheet paper, ragboard, or a piece of lightweight redboard the width of the back edge of the book and the length of the cover of the book. This piece of material is called the lettering strip and is used as a guide in lettering the cover.

The next step is to make up the cover, Process 21.

Process 21. Making Up the Cover

Place the back cover board on a piece of newspaper with the side marked "B" down and glue the exposed side. Put it on the binding material, allowing a ¾″ space on three sides as shown in Figure 81. Place the book on this cover with the square on two ends equal and the square on the front edge the width of a pencil line larger. In the same manner as above, glue the front cover and lay it in position on the book with the glued side up. Use the same square as on the back cover. Remember the squares on top and bottom are equal, but the square on the front edge is a bit larger.

Pull the binding material around the back of the book and over the glued surface of the front cover. Rub it evenly on the newly glued cover with the hand and bone folder. Open the cover and remove the book. Turn the cover over with the boards

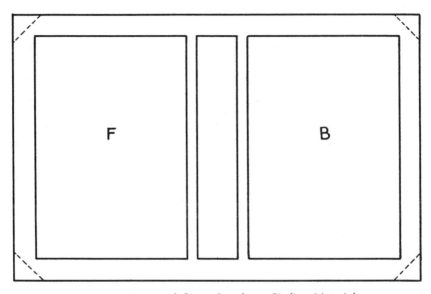

Fig. 81. Layout of Cover Boards on Binding Material

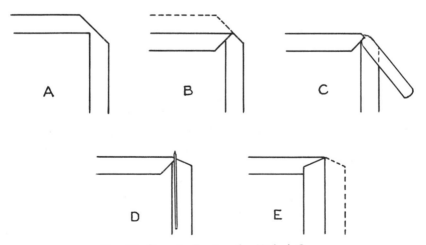

Fig. 82. Steps in Turning the Nicked Corner

down, and use the bone folder to rub the binding material which is over the boards. This removes air pockets and insures the sticking of the covers to the binding material.

If leather is used for binding material and bands are desired on the lettering strip, turn to Process 29 for applying the bands; otherwise, glue the lettering strip lightly and place it in the middle of the two covers as shown in Figure 81. Rub well with a bone folder.

If leather is being used for binding material, the workman must pare or skive the edges of the leather. This process may be done after the type of corners has been decided upon. Care should be taken to skive the corners as well as the edges when using leather.

Process 22. Turning Corners

Three types of corners are presented in this process. They are given in order of their occurrence in use, and care must be taken in the selection of the type in terms of the needs of the book. The first two are for square corners, while the third is a method of turning a round corner.

Turning the Nicked Corner

Cut all the corners off at an angle of 45° and about ⅜" from the corners of the boards, Figure 82, A. Glue all around the exposed edge of the binding material and the outside edges of the boards. Using the bone folder, turn in the top and bottom of the material first. With the pointed end of the bone folder, push the corners of the binding material against the edge of the board, forming a little "ear," Figure 82, C. Push the ear down and turn in the other two edges. After the edges are turned, lay the covers flat to dry and keep an old cover and wrapped brick or other weight on them. The covers should always dry flat and should never be put around the book to dry.

Turning the Library Corner

The library corner is one of the easiest to turn. It is used quite often by a few commercial binderies, and some people prefer this type to the nicked corner.

All four edges of the binding material are glued and the corners are turned in diagonally, forming an angle of 45° with the cover boards, Figure 83, **B**. Crease the material around the corners with a bone folder. After the four corners have been turned, the four edges are turned up and over. A bit of glue may be applied to the finished side of coated fabrics to hold the corner down.

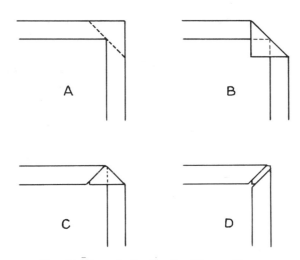

Fig. 83. Steps in Turning the Library Corner

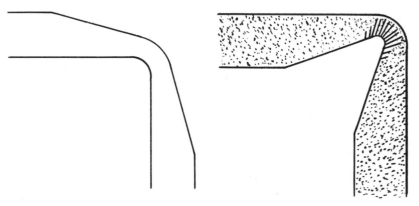

Fig. 84. Trimming Layout
for Picked-In Corner

Fig. 85. Completed
Picked-In Corner

Turning the Picked-In Corner

If round corners are desired, the outside corners of the cover boards must have previously been rounded. Cut the corners of the binding material as shown in Figure 84, leaving at least a 3⁄8″ margin at the corner.

Glue the four edges of binding material around the cover boards, and turn them in, leaving the corners open. Use a scratch awl to "pick-in" or fold in the extra material around the corner, Figure 85. After each corner is picked-in, use a hammer to flatten out the material.

Chapter 10

Lettering, Casing-In, and Finishing

Process 23. Lettering Full and Quarter Bindings

Materials and Equipment

Egg sizing
Coated-fabric sizing
Gold leaf
Imitation foil leaf
Type stick
Type (brass preferred)
Lettering machine
Hand pallet
Dividers
Pen and ink
Electric pen

Procedure

If the book is to be lettered by machine, copy the title and the author of the book on a scrap of paper and fasten this to the outside of the front cover with gummed tape.

If the book is to be hand lettered, omit the above step until after the book is taken from the press, Process 26.

The following procedure does not apply to gingham, oil-cloth, or to other such materials; it deals only with full, quarter, half, and three-quarter bindings in coated fabrics, vinyl, buckram, or book cloth, and quarter-bound leather bindings.

124

All book covers must be sized before they are lettered. The sizing melts when it comes in contact with the hot type, forms a base, and causes the gold or foil to stick to the book. Size the entire portion of the material which is directly over the lettering strip of the covers. This avoids spotting. Impregnated fabrics are sized with a special size, while starch-filled fabrics and leather books are sized with egg sizing. (Formulas are given on page 58.)

Whether the lettering is done by machine or by hand, the type is set in a "stick," which is made of metal and is used by printers for setting up type. After the type for the book has been set up, the process of lettering is ready to be begun. Machine lettering is much easier for the beginner and is preferred to hand lettering. It is difficult for some people to letter by hand even after many years of experience. Remember if hand lettering, pen-and-ink lettering, or electric pen lettering is to be done, the book should be finished completely before it is lettered.

Machine Lettering

To save time, the switch on the lettering machine should be turned on and the pallet allowed to heat before starting to set type. After the type has been set, it is put into the hot pallet and clamped tightly (generally one line at a time). Take an impression without gold on a piece of soft cardboard and check for spelling with the *Title Page* of the book.

The cover is centered on the platform so that the line of type is not longer than the lettering strip is wide. Move the platform or gauge so that the line of lettering is put at the desired point. There are many styles of lettering (Figure 86) and the workman should follow the directions on the lettering strip or use his own judgment.

After the type has been firmly clamped and the pallet turned to lettering position, place a piece of gold or foil under the type and pull the handle so that an even impression will result. If the foil or gold does not stick, the type is not hot enough. If the gold remains around and in the letters after it has been wiped off with a piece of flannel, the type is too hot.

Where even spacing is desired, a hubagraph may be used. The hubagraph is a piece of equipment which will space the backs of books equally. On one end is an adjustable gauge which can be used to make the bottom edge wider than the other spaces. This space is usually ⅝″. If a hubagraph is not available, measure up ⅝″ from the bottom edge of the back of the cover and divide the remaining distance from this point to the top edge into five equal parts. Place a pencil mark at the four upper points. The title is placed in the second space from the top, while the volume number, date, or author should go into the next to the bottom space, Figure 87. Modern binding tends to break away from the formality of even spacing. The craftsman today, if he is not bound by traditional standards, is free to select his own type face and apply it according to his taste.

Fig. 86. Typical Layout of
Lettering on Full Binding

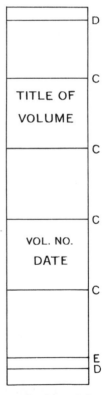

Fig. 87. Traditional Spacing
of Lettering on Full Binding

The workman should practice several times in order to get the proper amount of heat for the lettering and the correct impression. After taking a few practice impressions, it will soon be seen that the more type or the larger the type the more impression is necessary, and the less amount of type the less impression.

Hand Lettering

The book should be completed before it is lettered by hand. After the type has been set, it should be put into a hand pallet, which can be heated over a gas or an electric plate. The book is put into a finishers clamp so that the back edge is above the clamp about 1″. The head of the book should always be placed so that it comes to the left of the workman. A piece of gold leaf is removed from the gold book and placed on the cushion, where it is cut with a knife into strips a little larger than the lines of type. A special knife is best to use for this purpose, although it may also be done with a flat kitchen knife or thin steel strip.

Fig. 88. Lettering with a Hand Pallet

Care must be taken not to touch the blade with the hand. If it becomes oily, clean it with soap and water and dry with a clean cloth. The pallet is held in the right hand, and the gold is picked up from the gold cushion after the type has been wiped with a woolen rag which has been moistened with a small amount of olive oil. Hold the handle with one hand and steady the pallet with the other, using the oiled rag as a holder, Figure 88. The lettering is put in the same space as in machine lettering. Much practice is advised before attempting to letter a book in this manner, for the correct amount of impression and the proper heat are very important.

Pen and Ink Lettering

This operation takes place after the book is completed. A common pen holder and a waterproof ink of suitable color should be used for this purpose. Care should be taken in planning the lettering and the spacing of the lines.

Sometimes hand-lettered paper labels are used. These are first lettered and later applied to the book with glue.

Electric Pen Lettering

The metallic foils of different colors used in machine lettering may also be used when doing hand lettering with an electric pen. This pen is generally thermostatically controlled and is ready to use when hot. With a pencil, print on the wax-paper side of the foil the lettering that is to go on the book, being careful not to make any line longer than the width of the back edge of the book. Hold the paper or foil in position over the back edge and trace over the pencil lines with the point of the electric pen. Use slow, even strokes. Smooth materials are much easier to letter than rough materials. The books should be sized before lettering. Always varnish over the lettering to keep the foil from tarnishing. *Never use imitation gold on leather.*

Checking and Correcting Lettering

After the covers or the books have been lettered, remove the lettering slip from the cover or check the lettering on the back of the book with the *Title Page* of the book itself. If there is a mistake, correct it immediately by scratching out the lettering with a pointed tool, such as an awl or the point of a pair of dividers. Use a soft pencil eraser to remove the remaining gold. Set the type correctly and reletter.

If the cover has just been lettered, the book should be hung-in, Process 24.

Putting Lines on Books

If straight lines using various lengths of brass rule in the lettering machine are to be applied (**A**, **B**, **C**, **D**, and **E**, in Figures 86 and 87), this process should now be done. This will eliminate Process 27 if done at this time. Be sure the brass rule is no longer than the lettering strip is wide.

Process 24. Hanging-In the Book

The term "hanging-in" means fastening the back of the book to the lettering strip of the cover (notice that the endsheets and covers are not glued in this operation). This step is omitted in many commercially bound books but is possible here because of the spring back. On flat-stitched books the glue is applied directly to the flannel because the sewing does not permit the book to break away from the cover.

If the binding is full leather, follow Process 33 for instruction on "hanging-in."

Glue the entire space between the covers, including the lettering strip and joints. Do not glue the material turned in over the lettering strip at the top and bottom. Glue the entire back edge of the back of the book (which is the spring back or reinforcement material), starting in the center and gluing each way toward the top and bottom edges. This keeps the glue from running into the edges of the book. Set the book in place on the back cover with the correct square and pull the front cover over into its proper position. Use the long, flat edge of the bone folder to rub in the joints. Place a piece of paper over the back when rubbing so as not to scratch the lettering. The book is now ready to have its endsheets glued up, Process 25.

Process 25. Gluing Up the Endsheets

Open one cover, and with a "dry" glue brush (one which has been wiped free of all extra glue), glue the endsheet in the following manner:

Start from the center of the joint strip (**X**, Figure 89) and brush out each way on the joint strip and finish gluing the endsheet in a fan shape. Stroke the brush up and away from the endsheet each time to avoid getting glue into the edges of the book. Close the cover. Do not open the glued cover more than ³⁄₄″ for inspection. Turn the book over and glue the other endsheet. Close the cover in the same manner as the first. The book is now ready to be put in press, Process 26.

Process 26. Pressing and Cleaning the Book

Equipment

Grooved tins
Flat tins
Book press or combination press

The book should be put in press immediately following the gluing up of the endsheets. Pressing causes the endsheets to dry flat and keeps the covers from warping. The book should stay in press at least an hour, but a longer time is desirable. Allow it to remain in press as much as twenty-four hours if

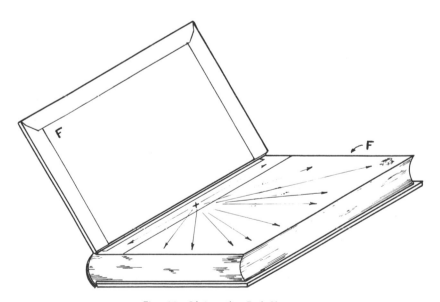

Fig. 89. Gluing the End Sheets

possible. If the book stays in press only one hour, put wrapped bricks on it after it is removed and allow to dry under this weight for twelve hours.

Procedure

First take two flat tins which are larger than the book and insert them between the newly glued endsheets. Place a piece of newspaper between each endsheet and the tin to pick up extra glue which may squeeze out. Remember, do not open the covers more than ¾" when inserting the tins. Obtain two tins with a turned edge which are to fit into the joints on the outside of the covers. These tins must be larger than the book. Fit the ridge of the tin into the joint and put the books in press. Check to be sure the turned edges are in the joints before running the press town tightly. If the workman uses a combination press, the flat tins are inserted as described and the press itself takes the place of the grooved tins.

After the book is taken out of the press it is ready to be cleaned. A piece of flannel dampened with water may be used when cleaning coated fabrics, but avoid allowing it to get on the endsheets and the gold lettering. Do not use water on buckram unless it is the waterproof type, as it will always fade or spot. However, the edges of the endsheets may be cleaned by using a piece of flannel dampened slightly in water. If an ordinary buckram-bound book happens to get glue on the cover, little can be done except to go ahead and sponge the spot and the entire cover. This is the reason for taking extreme care when binding books with a material which is not waterproof. The book is now ready for final inspection and rolling with gold on the back, Process 27.

Process 27. Rolling Coated Fabric and Buckram Books
Materials and Equipment

Roll gold
Book varnish
Finishing rolls

This process is for the workman who does not use brass rules to put on the lines as outlined in Process 23.

The following procedure is standard but may be varied to meet individual demands (this procedure does not apply to gingham, oilcloth, or other such materials). Apply suitable size to the backs of the books—for coated or impregnated fabrics, use the coated-fabric sizing; for starch filled fabrics, use egg sizing.

Coated Fabric Books

Place the book in the finisher's clamp or backer. Use the narrow finishing roll and heat it either on the gas or the electric plate. When it has heated to the proper temperature—hot, but not hot enough to burn leather—hold the handle with the right hand and turn the roll in a woolen rag lightly oiled with olive oil. Pull a strip of gold out over the leather on the gold cushion, and move the roll over the gold so that it will pick up the gold about three-fourths of the way around the roll. This will leave a space for holding the roll steady with the oiled rag when starting to apply the lines, Figure 90. The first lines should be rolled

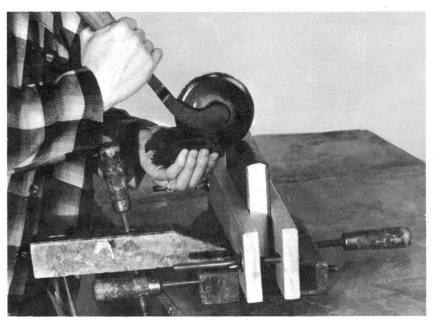

Fig. 90. Rolling a Book

¾" from the top and bottom edges on the back of the book (Figure 86, line **A**). A third line may be rolled ⅜" above the first at the bottom of the book as shown in Figure 86, line **B** (about ¾" from the bottom edge).

Buckram Books

If even spacing is desired on buckram books, a wide finishing roll is used and the lines should be rolled through the four points made by the hubagraph or dividers when the lettering was done (Figure 87, line **C**). Two more lines should be rolled ⅜" from the top and bottom edges (Figure 87, line **D**), and another should be rolled ⅜" above the first bottom line or ¾" above the bottom edge of the book (Figure 87, line **E**).

Applying Book Varnish

Book varnish should be applied to the entire back edge of the coated-fabric and buckram books. This may be applied with cotton or a piece of flannel and is done to protect the lettering and keep it from tarnishing. The book is now ready to go back to the library shelf.

Chapter 11

Quarter, Half, and Three-Quarter Bindings

Process 28. Cutting Binding Materials
Materials

Library morocco
Library cowhide
Coated fabric or buckram

NOTE: *If you are working with quarter, half, or three-quarter bindings you will proceed here after completing Process 19. You should have omitted all processes from 20 through 27.*

Quarter, half, and three-quarter bindings are more difficult than ordinary full binding. When leather is used for the back material and corners, it makes for a stronger type of binding and a better-looking book.

The first method of cutting materials for this type of binding is a *composite* one (Figure 91) which makes for ease in getting out materials in school or home workshops. The other methods which follow are traditional ones which actually determine the kind of binding and have all measurements in proportion to the size of the cover.

The beginner is advised to use the composite method and school shops will also find it most satisfactory. Those interested in following the age-old procedure developed in the craft of bookbinding should follow the traditional method. On large books the traditional method is more satisfactory because the larger the book the more binding material used.

134

Composite Method

Material for Back

Regardless of the type of material used—whether it be coated fabric, buckram, or leather—the following procedure should be observed when using the composite method:

Make a paper pattern 2½″ longer than the book or 2″ longer than the boards. Its width is the thickness of the back edge of the book plus 3½″. Use this measurement for quarter, half, or three-quarter bindings.

Material for Corners

Quarter-bound books do not have corners, but half and three-quarter bindings do. Omit this step when binding a quarter-bound book.

The paper pattern for corners should be made as follows:

Cut a 3½″ square diagonally, and cut off the top of the triangle thus formed 2″ above the base, Figure 92.

Care must be taken to obtain the correct color and kind of material. This information is generally specified by the owner. Always cut a paper pattern the exact size of the material for each book, to insure less waste in cutting. Powder around the paper pattern on the leather or trace around the pattern on coated fabrics or buckram. Regardless of the size of the book,

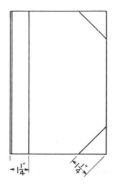

Fig. 91. Layout of
Composite Binding

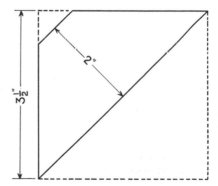

Fig. 92. Corner Pattern
for Composite Binding

four corners of the size given above should be cut for half or three-quarter bindings only when the workman is using the composite method.

Traditional Method

This method calls for accurate measuring and more time spent in getting out materials.

Material for Back

Cut a paper pattern 2″ longer than the cover and width determined as follows:

Quarter-Bound Books

The width of the binding material used for the back edge extends onto the two sides of the book one-eighth the width of the cover board, Figure 93. Therefore, cut the paper pattern for quarter-bound books as follows:

To one-fourth the width of the cover board, add the thickness of the back edge of the book plus 1″ for the joints.

Half-Bound Books

The width of the binding material extends over the side of the covers one-fourth the width of the cover boards as shown in Figure 94. Cut the width of the back material as follows:

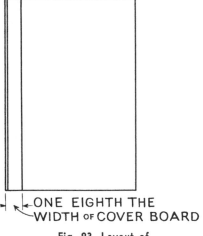

ONE EIGHTH THE WIDTH OF COVER BOARD

Fig. 93. Layout of Quarter-Bound Book

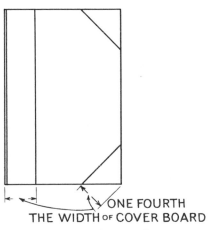

ONE FOURTH THE WIDTH OF COVER BOARD

Fig. 94. Layout of Half-Bound Book

To one-half the width of the cover board, add the width of the back edge of the book plus 1″.

Three-Quarter-Bound Books

The width of the binding material extends onto the side of the covers one-third the width of the boards, Figure 95. Cut the width of the back material as follows:

To two-thirds the width of the cover boards, add the width of the back edge of the book plus 1″.

Material for Corners

The pattern for corners is made in the following manner:

Cut a 6″ to 8″ square from a piece of paper. Draw the two diagonals from corner to corner and cut the square in two pieces on one of the diagonals (**XY**, Figure 96). Measure in on the pencil line $\frac{5}{8}$″ from the corner; draw a line parallel to the long edge and cut off, Figure 96. From point **A**, Figure 96, measure the width of the corners as follows:

1. For half-bound books measure from point **A**, Figure 96, on the line **AB** one-fourth the width of the cover boards plus $\frac{3}{4}$″ (distance **H**, Figure 96). Draw a line parallel to the base and cut off. With the pattern thus formed, cut four identical corners.

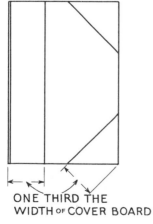

ONE THIRD THE
WIDTH OF COVER BOARD

Fig. 95. Layout of
Three-Quarter-Bound Book

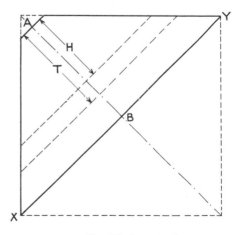

Fig. 96. Layout of
Traditional Corner

2. For three-quarter bound books measure from point **A**, Figure 96, one-third the width of the cover boards plus $\frac{3}{4}''$ (distance **T**, Figure 96). Draw a line parallel to the base **XY** and cut off. Using this pattern, cut four identical corners.

Process 29. Making Up Lettering Strip

Generally, bands are not applied to quarter-bound books. They are usually applied on half and three-quarter bindings when leather is used. Any number of bands may be used on the lettering strip. Two, four, or five bands are generally used. The following instructions are for four bands, as this is the most common:

If equal spaces are desired, measure up $\frac{5}{8}''$ from the bottom and draw a line, Figure 97, **A**. Divide the remaining space into five equal parts and draw lines across the lettering strip, Figure 97, **B**. This may be done with a pair of dividers or a rule.

Cut four pieces of band material from a lightweight cardboard or equivalent. These pieces are $\frac{3}{16}''$ in width and about $\frac{1}{16}''$ thick; their length is equal to the width of the lettering strip. The number of bands used is optional with the craftsman.

The ragboard should be glued on one side and the four bands should be placed above the four lines which were just drawn, Figure 97, **B**.

Press the strips carefully with the fingers and allow to dry for ten or fifteen minutes.

Fig. 97. Layout of Lettering Strip

Process 30. Making Up Quarter, Half, and Three-Quarter Covers

After the binding materials have been cut and the bands applied to the lettering strip (in half, three-quarter, and full bindings) pare or skive around all the edges of the leather, including the corners. If the book is to be quarter-bound, it will not have corners or bands on the lettering strip, unless otherwise specified. If material other than leather is used, do not put bands on the lettering strip.

Applying the Corners

On the first few books, it is advisable to place a check mark on the outside of the covers where the leather corner is to be glued (half and three-quarter bindings only). Glue two corners and place them on one cover over the check marks, allowing 5/8" for turn-in on the two edges. A nicked corner is generally used with leather, so this procedure is presented. (If another type of corner is desired, refer to Process 22.) Using the bone folder, turn in the top and bottom edges of the corners. Take the pointed end of the bone folder and push in the corners, forming an "ear" (Process 22). Push this ear down and turn in the remaining edges. This forms the nicked corner. Apply the other two corners in the same manner.

Applying the Back Binding Piece

If the composite method was used in cutting the binding materials for a half-bound book, use the following procedure:

Glue 1¼" on the outside of the covers along the edge opposite the corners. It is best to measure and mark a guideline. Place the long edge of the leather which was cut for the back over the glued portion of the back cover. Turn this cover over so that the outside is toward the table. Place the back of the book on this cover in the proper position, allowing a one-fourth larger square on the front edge than on the top and bottom edges. Place the front cover on the book in the same position as the first, and draw on the leather around the back and over the glued portion. Open the cover and lay it flat. Remove the book. The lettering strip should now be applied.

If the traditional method was used in cutting the binding materials, one of the following procedures must be used:

Quarter-Bound Books

Measure on the front and back cover boards one-eighth their width and mark lines indicating this distance along the length of the cover. Glue this space, which is one-eighth the width of the cover, and place the piece of back material over the glued portion of the back cover. Place the book in its proper position, the front cover in place, and draw on the piece of back material over the front cover. Do not worry if it extends over the line, as the siding-up material will cover any irregularities.

Half-Bound Books

Measure on the front and back cover boards one-fourth their width and mark lines indicating this distance along the outside edge of the cover boards opposite the corners. The corners were applied in the first section of this process. Glue this distance and place the back piece of material over the glued portion of the back cover. Turn the cover over so that the finished side of the binding material is down, and place the book in its proper position. Place the front cover on top of the book in its correct position and draw on the piece of back material. Do not be concerned if it extends over the line, as the siding-up material will cover any irregularities. Open the cover and remove the book. The lettering strip should now be applied.

Three-Quarter-Bound Books

Measure on the front and back cover boards one-third of their width, and mark lines this distance along the edge of the cover boards, opposite the corners, which have been applied. Glue this distance and place the piece of back material over the glued portion of the back cover. Turn the cover over so that the outside is down, and place the book in proper position with a one-fourth larger square on the front edge than on the top and bottom edges. Place the front cover board on the book in this same position and draw on the piece of back material over the glued portion. Do not be concerned if it extends over the pencil line, as the siding-up material will cover any irregularities. Open the cover and remove the book. The lettering strip is now ready to be applied.

Applying the Lettering Strip

If material other than leather is being used for these types of bindings, do not use bands on the lettering strips. Usually bands are not applied to the lettering strip of quarter-bound books even when leather is used as the binding material. Glue and apply the plain lettering strip as described in Process 21.

Glue the banded side of the lettering strip, if it is to have bands, and place it on the wrong side of the binding material between the covers so that it is centered. Be sure that the large space on the lettering strip is at the bottom of the cover.

If bands are being used on a leather book, they must be raised. Turn the book over so that the finished side of the leather is up, and rub the back of the entire piece of leather with a clean, stiff-bristle brush. Using a grooved stick whose grooves are a little wider than the bands, rub over the bands, causing them to stand out on the leather. Avoid running the grooved stick into the joints of the cover.

Making the Covers Ready for Lettering

Copy the title, volume number, the date, and the name of the author on a scrap piece of paper, fasten this to the outside of the front cover with gummed tape. The cover is now ready to be lettered. If it is a quarter-bound book, turn to Process 23 for instruction. If it is a full, half, or three-quarter leather binding, follow Process 31.

Process 31. Lettering Half, Three-Quarter, and Full Leather Bindings

The entire back of the leather must be sized with egg sizing. Care must be taken in applying the size, as too much gives as poor results as too little—a thin coat is sufficient.

Machine Lettering

The type is set in a "stick," which is made of metal and is used by printers for this purpose. The pallet on the lettering machine should be heated to the proper temperature. It is better to stamp the ornaments, or "center stamps," first if they are to be used. These ornaments are sometimes put into the first, third, and fifth spaces (Figure 98) when equal spacing is used. The cover is centered under the pallet and the table is adjusted so that the stamping will be done in the proper place. Hold a piece of gold leaf under the type and over the back of the book and pull the handle enough to secure a clear impression. If the gold does not stick to the leather, the type is not hot enough. If too much gold sticks around and in the letters after it has been rubbed off, the machine is too hot.

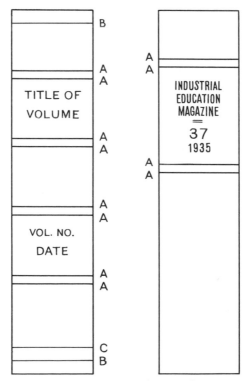

Fig. 98. Layouts of Lettering Strips

Experience will give the workman a sense of correct heat and the proper amount of impression. Practice on a scrap piece of leather before attempting to letter the book. Always use pure gold leaf on leather. Imitation gold will tarnish.

The title, generally in two lines, is next lettered and goes in the second space. The volume number, the date, and sometimes the part number are placed in the space next to the bottom, Figure 98. Occasionally the author's name is lettered in this space if the book is not a volume of magazines. After the book has been lettered, the heads are turned, Process 32.

If the book is to be hand lettered with a hand pallet, an electric pen, or pen and ink, follow the directions as given in Process 23.

Putting on Lines

If the workman has various lengths of brass rule, lines may be applied to the back of the book by putting the brass rule in the pallet and using the lettering machine. Be sure the lines are not longer than the lettering strip is wide. If these lines are applied now, omit Process 35.

Apply a line on each side of the bands as shown by lines A, Figure 98. Two lines, lines B, are applied ⅜″ from the top and bottom edges. Line C, Figure 98, is applied about ¾″ from the bottom edge.

Process 32. Turning-In the Heads

The term "turning-in the head" of a leather binding means the turning over of the leather at the top and bottom edges of the back cover. These two ends of leather extending beyond the lettering strip must be glued and allowed to dry a few minutes to permit the glue to set. With the bone folder and fingertips, turn the leather so the two edges will stick to the covers only (it is not permitted to stick to the lettering strip yet). Working against a thick rule or piece of binders board, push the leather down against the lettering strip, leaving a "bead" or raised edge along the fold. This bead is for appearance only, so that it will fit tightly against the headband and turn slightly over the edge of the band. Sometimes this bead is made by putting in a piece of heavy cord the width of the lettering strip to facilitate raising it. This is unnecessary if the above instructions are carefully followed. The book should be hung-in to this cover immediately to help the forming or setting the heads, Process 33.

Process 33. Hanging-In the Book

If material other than leather is used, follow instructions in Process 24.

Glue the back edge of the book and the entire lettering strip (including the joints) between the cover boards. Care must be taken not to glue the leather at the top and bottom of the lettering strip as excess glue will show after the book is fastened into the cover. Lay the book in position, being sure that the back of the book is on the back cover. Pull the other cover into position. Use the bone folder lengthwise when rubbing in the joints. Grooved tins should be placed in the joints and pressed five minutes. While the book is between the tins, use the flat side of the bone folder and "set" the head over the headbands, which gives the book a more finished appearance, Figure 99.

The cover is ready to be "sided-up," Process 34.

Fig. 99. Setting the Heads on Leather Bindings

Process 34. The Siding-Up Process

Two pieces of siding-up material should be cut from either coated fabric, book cloth, or buckram and should harmonize in color with the leather or other binding material. This material is always cut 2″ longer than the cover board and the same width as the cover board. Before this material is applied, one of the following procedures should be followed, depending on the kind of binding.

Siding-Up Half and Three-Quarter Bindings

Find the smallest leather corner on the cover, measure in ⅛″ on the leather, and draw a pencil line diagonally across the corner, Figure 100. Find the place where the leather of the back extends on to the boards the least distance and measure in on the leather ⅛″ at this point, Figure 100, **XY**. Turn the

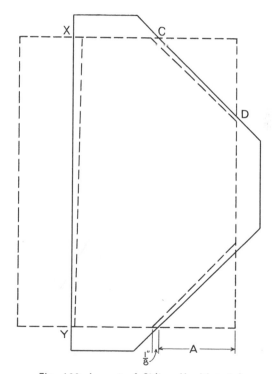

Fig. 100. Layout of Siding Up Material

book over and mark the same distance on the other cover. This same distance should now be marked at the other end of each cover and the points connected with a pencil line, Figure 100, **XY**. Place the siding-up material along the back in position (along the line just made) until the same amount of turn-in exists on both ends. Turn the material back over the marked corner until it is even with the pencil line, **CD**, Figure 100. Crease this material even with the line. Place both pieces of the siding-up material together, fold across the narrow way, and cut the four corners at once across the creased line. Either the board shears or hand shears may be used for the purpose. Glue the unfinished side of these siding-up pieces and place them in their proper position on the two covers as shown by the dotted lines in Figure 100. Lift the cover which is on top and turn in the three extending edges, turning the top and bottom ones first. Turn the book over and fold in the edges on the other cover in the same manner.

The book is now ready to have the endsheets glued up and put into press, Process 25.

Siding-Up Quarter Bindings

Find the place where the leather on the back extends over onto the cover the least distance and measure in on the leather ⅛″ at this point. Turn the book over and mark this same distance on the other cover. This distance should also be marked at the other end of each cover and the points connected with a pencil line. The points may be determined by using a pair of dividers or a rule.

Glue the unfinished side of the two pieces of siding-up material previously cut and place them in their proper position (along the line just drawn), with the same amount of turn-in existing at both edges of the cover. Cut the corners according to the type desired and turn the edges, following instructions given in Process 22.

The endsheets are now ready to be glued up and the book put into press. See Processes 25 and 26.

Process 35. Rolling a Half Goat Book

If the lines have already been applied by using brass rule in the lettering machine, Process 31, omit these instructions.

Rolling the Book

Size the entire back of the leather over the lettering strip with egg sizing.

Place a narrow roll over an electric plate or gas burner and allow it to get hot (not so hot as to burn a piece of leather). When it has reached the proper temperature, take a woolen rag to which some olive oil has been applied and turn the roll in the rag. Pull a strip of gold out over the leather on the gold cushion and move the roll over it so that it will pick up gold about three-fourths of the way around the roll. This will leave a space for holding the roll steady with the oily rag.

Roll a line on each side of the bands as shown in Figure 98, line **A**. Lines should also be rolled ⅜″ from the top and bottom of the book, Figure 98, line **B**. Another line should be rolled at the bottom ⅜″ above the first or ¾″ above the bottom edge, Figure 98, line **C**.

While all decoration will probably be specified, the craftsman can see that the back can be made as plain or ornate as desired. Care must be taken not to overdo this type of work.

Remember to use pure gold leaf on leather.

Final Inspection and Varnishing the Book

The leather, including the corners, should be treated with book varnish or book lacquer. The book is now ready to be placed on the library shelf.

Part III

Special Techniques and Problems

Chapter 12

The Bookbinder's Records

Many record problems will confront the workman, be he home craftsman, school librarian or commercial binder. Books will find their way to his bindery from many sources—churches, public or school libraries, lodges, classroom teachers and other individuals. Experience has shown that it is necessary to keep an accurate record of these volumes as they come in, and for that purpose the record sheet, Figure 101, is suggested. Several books may be listed on this card. If a number of books come from a library, it is suggested that a form similar to Figure 102 be printed for the librarian to give directions to the bindery. One of these slips should be put in each book.

This record should be filled out by the person bringing books to the bindery and care should be taken to be sure he has indicated the type of binding desired and the kind and color of material to be used. This procedure tends to eliminate both misunderstanding and confusion. Special cases, such as permission to combine parts of old, incomplete books into a few complete volumes, should be so indicated on the blank.

Records of Individual Books

After books are received in the bindery, it is desirable to keep a record of each book so that it may be located at any time. In a school bindery it is often necessary to find a book for a teacher or student doing research or reference work, and the

BINDERY BOOK LIST

Date _____

Name _____
    Individual ordering the binding of the following books

Materials Charged to _____

Title of Book	Color of Binding	Number of Books Received	Number of Books Discarded	Number of Books Returned	Date of Completion
Total					

Fig. 101. Bindery Book List

BINDING SLIP

Lettering:

_____

_____

(Title)

_____

_____

(Author)

_____

Special Instructions:

_____

Color:

_____   Buckram

_____   Coated Fabric

_____   Book Cloth

_____   Leather

Type of Binding:

_____   Full

_____   Half

_____   Quarter

Fig. 102. Librarian's Binding Slip

record card shown in Figure 103 is most satisfactory for this purpose. It lists the student or workman doing the binding and his locker number, which permits the book to be found immediately.

Fill in the following: The date the books were received by the binder, title of book or books, color of binding desired, and number of volumes. The other columns on the card will be filled out by the person in charge when the books are completed. When the card is filled out, return it to the record box provided for that purpose.

This card can be filed away when the books are completed to assist the teacher or foreman in compiling annual reports, achievement of individual students or binders, or for any other purpose.

Analyzing the Job to be Done

If the method of shop organization requires that individual records be kept, the filling out of that record is the first step. This step is omitted where the card system is not used.

The next procedure is to determine exactly what must be done to the book. In some instances this has already been determined, especially if the book comes from the library with

RECORD CARD

Card Number_____

Name _____
Person responsible for binding

Date	Title of Books	Color of Binding	Number of Books	To be filled in by instructor		
				O.K.	Initials	Date of Completion
Total						

Fig. 103. Bindery Record Card

a binding slip (Figure 102) or specific instructions for binding. However, if no instruction accompanies the volume, or if the owner is undecided as to how the book should be bound, the binder must make the decision in terms of the problems stated in Chapter 2.

The binder must determine exactly what is to be done to the book and then, following the step-by-step procedure of the instructions, proceed with those operations.

A repair job is usually not as extensive a procedure as when the book is to be rebound. It may only need a strip on the back of the cover or a minor gluing or sewing operation. When it is to be put back into the old cover, usually it must have new endsheets or new sewing. A complete rebinding includes new endsheets, new cover, and usually new sewing. The binding slip also should indicate the kind of binding the book is to have and the color in which it is to be bound.

BOOK RECORD CARD

Title of Volume _____

Color and Material _____

Index _____	Front trim _____
Sewing _____	Bottom trim _____
Endsheets _____	Top trim _____
Stipple _____	Number of board _____
Headbands _____	Height of covers _____
Cost of binding _____	Kind of corners _____
Bind: _____	

Fig. 104. Individual Book Record Card (3″ x 5″)

Other Records

One of the most important and useful records a binder may use is an individual book-record card. This card, Figure 104, should be used for all magazines and for those books which are parts of sets of books. It contains information on color and kind of material, color of endsheets, placement of index, method of sewing, choice of headbands, kind of corners, and cost. It also contains the finished size of the book with regard to front trim, bottom trim, and top trim; the thickness of board; length of covers; and whether the edges are to be stippled or not. At the bottom of the card, space is allowed for any additional information which is necessary for binding the book.

This record makes it possible for the binder to match books within a set as to size and color each year without consulting a finished volume. In order to match the lettering of these volumes, it is recommended that a "sample" be lettered on a scrap piece of binding material at the same time the book

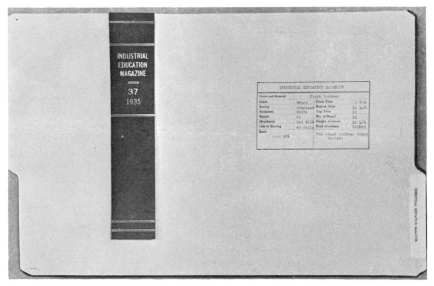

Fig. 105. Folder Used for Filing Lettering and Binding Information

cover is lettered. If possible, make the sample from the same material as the cover and approximately the same size as the lettering strip. This may be stapled on the inside of a manila folder and filed away near the lettering machine, Figure 105. The information on the individual book-record card may be kept on the other side of the folder, to provide for duplicate information if the card is lost.

Another method used to match the lettering on volumes of books which are alike is by means of a "rub" of the back of the book. A piece of $8\frac{1}{2}'' \times 11''$ typing paper is used for this purpose. The "rub" is made by holding the piece of paper over the lettering, flush at the top, and rubbing a soft pencil on the paper covering the entire back of the book. The information on the individual book-record card may also be printed, written, or stamped on this sheet.

With the above records, it is easy to keep each volume of a set of magazines exactly like the previously bound volumes.

Chapter 13

Mass Production in the Hand Bindery

Single volumes or sets of two or three volumes present individual problems to the workman and must be bound as a special job. However, when ten or more volumes of the same size are to be bound there are several ways of saving time and material.

In school shops especially, or in any other bindery where more than one person will be working, a "cooperative" or "production" setup may be utilized to best advantage. All the different operations may be distributed among the various workmen. Two people, or a crew of twenty-two persons, may work on this plan; one or two lines can be organized and the services of many hands employed. While one person is tearing down, another may be preparing endsheets, and still another cutting joint strips. Two or three can make up endsheets as soon as they are cut and another one or two may apply them to the book. In this manner, punching, sewing, turning back endsheets, applying reinforcement material (flannel or muslin), trimming, rounding and backing, cutting covers, cutting lettering strips, and cutting the binding material (coated fabrics, buckram, et cetera) may follow. Care must be taken at the time the books are to be trimmed that they are cut to the same size and that no one disturbs the gauge during this operation.

The educational value to the student through observation of the saving of time, and its economic implications, will readily be seen. On this cooperative basis most time is saved in making up the covers, and the full benefit of the plan can best be realized if a systematic procedure is observed. (It is best that most participants have had some previous binding experience; each workman may perform one operation or a series of operations before passing the work on to the next individual; in this manner, much time is saved.)

The binding of school annuals will not differ from the binding of other books except in the fact that the joint strip is omitted (using a folded endsheet) and the endsheets are glued or pasted to the book. Here the sewing on of endsheets is omitted.

Making Up Covers on a Production Basis (Materials Previously Cut)

1. The binding material is glued solid. Brush glue from the center toward the edges.

2. Place the back cover board in position on the right side of the material with ¾″ margin on three sides, Figure 106.

3. Place a book on the back cover board so that an equal "square"[1] is formed on the front, top, and bottom edges.

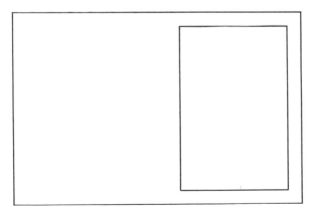

Fig. 106. Placement of Back Cover Board on Binding Material

[1] Definition of "square" is on page 117.

4. Place the front cover board on the book so that it too has an equal square on the front, top, and bottom edges. Much care must be taken to see that an equal square is formed on the front edges of the covers because it is at this point that many errors occur; an incorrect placement of covers may cause a number of serious troubles later.

5. With the right hand holding the cover board in place, draw the binding material over the front cover.

6. Open the cover and return the book to the stack.

7. Place lettering strip exactly in center of space between the two covers.

8. Cut the corners and turn back edges as described in Process 22.

9. The exact placement of the two covers was determined with the completion of Step 5. Time will be saved with the construction of a casemaking gauge. Refer to Chapter 3, page 42, for a description of this gauge and make one to suit the requirements of the job.

10. See that the gauge is set to the exact width of the distance between the two covers.

11. Glue another piece of binding material.

12. Place a back cover in position as described in Step 2.

13. Place the gauge on the glued binding material so that the right side of the gauge is against the inside and top of the back cover.

14. Place the front cover against the left side of the gauge. Be sure that the top of the gauge and the top of the front cover are in line.

15. Place the lettering strip in the space between covers as in Step 7.

16. Cut corners and turn edges as in Step 8.

17. This cover was made with the use of the gauge and a check must now be made with several books to be sure it is accurate. Take a book from two or three different places in the stacks and try each of them in the cover, being sure that the square on the top, bottom, and front edges of each is equal. If there is too much square, set the gauge smaller; if the square is too small, open the gauge. If the gauge is proved to be accurate, work can begin at once.

This procedure may be set up in various ways so that workers share responsibilities. As the last step, someone should be responsible for checking the corners and properly stacking the covers. To prevent getting glue on the backs of covers they should be stacked so that outsides and insides face together, which simply requires that every other one be turned face side over. They should be kept under pressure until dry. Lacking better means, a few bricks or weights placed on top of the pile will prevent curling or warping.

The covers are now lettered, if that is to be done. Later the book is hung in and pressed in standing press, using brass-bound boards if available. See Figure 107.

Special Problems in Binding School Annuals

The entire procedure of a mass-production job assignment may be followed. However, endsheet make-up and the type of

Fig. 107. Standing Press

sewing may differ according to the requirements of the book and should be carefully selected by the instructor. If the annual is printed in the school printshop or by the local printer, it can be wire stitched. Since this book sees its hardest use only during the "autograph signing period," the folded endsheet may be used with a joint strip omitted. This saves joint-strip cost, a minor item, and much time in make-up. If the annual is printed in sections and the job is not a hurried one, it may be loom sewed in the bindery in place of being wire stitched. After the book has been either sewed or stitched, the following procedure may be followed:

Making Up and Applying Endsheets

1. Cut two endsheets for each book—the exact length and two times the width of the book. The sheet should be cut so that the grain or "easy" way of the fold runs lengthwise of the book.

2. The sheets should be folded in the middle so that they are the exact size of the annual.

3. Glue one side of the folded edge of each endsheet 1/4". Eight or ten may be glued at one time with the use of a tipping strip.

4. Place an endsheet on the book, glued side down, so that the folded edge comes flush with the back edge of the book.

5. If the book has been loom sewed, the ends of the tapes and cords are glued to the endsheet. Fray the ends of the cords before gluing, as described in Process 11. Glue only one side at a time; after it is dry, turn the book over and glue the other side.

6. Cut reinforcement material (muslin or super cloth) the thickness of the back of the annual plus 3", and 1/2" shorter than the book.

7. Working around the edge of a table, glue the back of each book and 1" of the endsheet of each book (along the back). Turn the book over and glue 1" of the other endsheet, the back of the book remaining out over the edge of the table.

8. As rapidly as the books are glued, another workman can apply the muslin cut in Step 6. Center it on the back of the book and fold over onto the glued endsheets. Allow to dry.

9. Trim the books and follow exactly the procedure listed in this chapter on making up and applying covers.

Commercial Covers

Occasionally the financial committee of the school annual will feel that there are sufficient funds to have the cover embossed by a commercial company. If this is to be done, several procedures will have to be observed.

1. The covers should be made up several weeks in advance of the time when the books need to be bound. This can easily be done from a dummy furnished by the printer. This dummy should be made up using the exact paper, the same endsheet material, and should be sewed in the same manner as the finished book. It should contain the exact number of pages and be trimmed to the finished size. The book should not be changed in any way after the covers are made up.

2. If the cover itself is not to be "grained" in the embossing process, use any material desired. A coated fabric is recommended.

3. If a special grain is later to be embossed, use a skiver-grain coated fabric in making up the covers. This material has no decorative grain and is less expensive.

4. If the title, an ornamental panel, or the entire book is to be embossed, use a glue made from a mixture of 50 percent hard flake glue and 50 percent flexible glue. This is desirable because of the pressure and heat used in the embossing process.

The firm which is to do the embossing should be consulted as to the possibilities of color and grain effect obtainable through this process.

Chapter 14

Binding Bibles and Other DeLuxe Bindings

Deluxe binding differs from full leather binding in that the cover is flexible, it extends and is bent over the book. The endsheets are usually made up of a skiver or moire-grain coated fabric, though any other grain or material may be used.

Determining the Type of Sewing Necessary

1. If the sewing is in good shape, the endsheets may be applied or sewed on as soon as they are made up, as in Process 2.

2. If the sewing is broken but the sections are in good shape (no single loose pages), the book may be loom sewed.

3. If the book has many loose pages, it will have to be punched and sewed using the overcast method.

Making Up Endsheets for a Bible (Not Loom Sewed)

If the book is ready to have endsheets applied (Step 1, above), or if the overcast method is used (Step 3, above), the following procedure should be followed:

1. Cut two pieces of white bond or ledger paper the exact size of the book.

2. Glue one edge of these sheets ¼″ and place against front and back of Bible, with glued edges even with the back of the book.

161

3. Cut two pieces of light moire-grain coated fabric (or other endsheet material) the same length as the book and twice the width of the book plus 1″.

4. Glue one white sheet (which was applied in step 2) solid and place wrong side of selected endsheet flush with the front, top, and bottom edges. This permits it to extend over the back of the book.

5. Fold the endsheet back over the book so that the crease is even with the back edge of the book. It now extends 1″ over the front edge of the book.

6. Follow the instructions in Process 3 for applying endsheets. If sewed-on endsheets are preferred, see Processes 7, 10, and 13 for punching, sewing, and turning back endsheets.

Making Up Endsheets for Loom Sewing

1. Saw out the book, following directions in Process 8.

2. Cut two pieces of sign cloth (obtainable at any dry-goods store) or white stay cloth, 2″ wide and the length of the book, for joint strips.

3. Cut two pieces of bond or ledger paper the same length as the book and 1″ narrower than the book.

4. Glue each of these sheets ¼″ along the long edge and place a joint strip (cut in step 2) over this glued edge so that it extends out from the sheet 1¾″.

5. Measure in ⅜″ from the outer edge of the joint strip and fold over. The fold comes on the "paper" side of the joint strip.

6. Take the front section and the back section from the book. Glue ⅜″ along the folded edge of the front of the back section and ⅜″ along the folded edge of the back of the front section and apply the folded joint strip so that the white endsheets come to the outside of the front and back sections.

7. Loom sew the book according to directions in Process 11.

8. Cut two coated-fabric endsheets the length of the book and twice its width and fold them in the middle, making them the exact size of the book. The finished side should be folded in.

9. Glue white bond paper and exposed portion of joint strip on outside and place endsheet over it so that folded edge is even with the back of the book.

10. In like manner, glue on the other endsheet.

11. Fray ends of cords and glue down. Glue down tapes. When the cords and tapes are dry, turn the book and repeat on other endsheet.

Forwarding

Regardless of type of sewing, follow the instructions in applying reinforcement material, trimming, rounding, and backing, and applying headbands and spring back material. If the book has a gold or red edge which is to be preserved, omit the trimming step.

Cutting and Making Up Covers

1. Cutting covers for deluxe-bound Bibles follows the same rule as other books (Process 19) with the exception that flexible redboard is used in place of binders board. Round the four corners which come at the front of the book, not to exceed a ¼″ radius.

2. Cut two pieces of coach wadding the size of each redboard cover for padding.

3. Cut two pieces of muslin or super cloth 2″ longer and 2″ wider than the cover.

4. Glue one side of each cover 1″ around all four edges.

5. Place the padding in the center of the muslin (or super cloth) and place the cover over the padding, glued side up.

6. Turn the four edges of muslin up over the glued edges of the redboard cover and cut away the fullness of muslin which sticks up at the corners.

7. Make a paper pattern for the leather in the following manner: Place the covers on the book and put it on a piece of paper so that it has a "turn-in" equal to the thickness of the Bible on three edges. Pull the paper around and over the top cover, leaving the thickness of the book on the fourth edge. This provides a full overlapping. If the semi-overlapping effect is desired, use *half* the thickness of the book for a turn-in.

8. Place paper pattern on leather and powder around it, using a piece of cotton or blackboard eraser. Cut leather on powdered line.

9. Pare or skive all four edges on wrong side not to exceed ¼″.

10. On the unfinished side of the leather, mark the exact position of each cover by placing the covers on the book in their proper position and forming an equal square on three sides. Place the book and covers in this position on the leather so that the turn-in on three edges is the same. Mark position of back cover with a lead pencil. Draw over and in a like manner mark position of front cover.

11. Cut a joint strip, from ragboard or endsheet paper, the width of the back edge of the book and the length of the cover.

12. Spread a thin coat of glue on a piece of newspaper over a space larger than a cover. Place back cover in the glue with reinforcement material down.

13. Lift the cover and place in marked position on right-hand side of leather.

14. Place the book on the back cover, being sure the square is equal on front, top, and bottom edges.

15. Glue newspaper and place front cover in glued spot as in Step 12 above.

16. Lift from glue and place in position on book, being sure again the square is correct.

17. Draw leather over, holding front cover in position with right hand.

18. Open leather cover and remove book.

19. Glue lettering strip and position exactly between the two covers.

20. The pared edge of the cover is now ready to be folded up and turned in. To determine the location of this fold, find the center of the distance which the leather extends beyond the cover and mark a point. From this middle point measure in toward the covers $\frac{3}{16}''$. Draw a line this distance from the covers all the way around the "turn-in" on the outside of the covers.

21. Using a piece of tin or a thin metal rule as a straight-edge, lift leather up on this line, fold over, and tap lightly with a hammer.

22. The pared edge of the leather should now extend over the edges of the covers about $\frac{3}{8}''$.

23. Cut the corners ¼″ above the fold as shown in Figure 108.

24. Glue the leather around the covers and fold over all four edges. Use the bone folder to set the crease along the edges of the covers and to remove all air pockets.

25. Use the scratch awl to "pick in" the corners as shown in Figure 109. (See Process 22.) This should make a slightly rounded corner.

Fig. 108. Cutting a Bible Corner

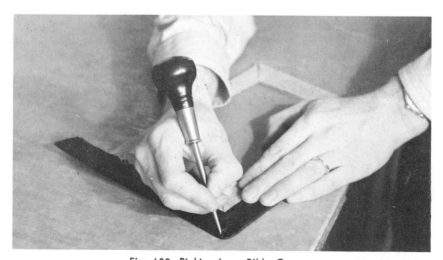

Fig. 109. Picking-In a Bible Corner

26. Letter according to directions in the instructions, Process 23.

27. Lightly glue over the lettering strip and the space between the covers. Glue the back edge of the book (the spring back). Work from center toward edges in both cases.

28. Place the book in position on the back cover and draw the front cover over into its proper position. Put a piece of newspaper over the back of the book and rub with the hand.

29. Intstead of using pressing tins after the endsheets have been glued, cut four pieces of lightweight cardboard (or No. 40 chipboard) ½" larger each way than the covers.

30. Glue the endsheets as described in Process 25.

31. Place two pieces of the cardboard between the front and back endsheets. The other two pieces are put on the outside of the book.

32. Place the book in press, tighten and loosen the press alternately several times, and remove the book.

33. Put the book away to dry with one or two bricks on top of the cardboard for weights. Allow book to dry at least 24 hours.

34. Cut several long strips of spring-back paper, each the width of the length of the cover, less 2". Glue these pieces together, making one strip 4' or 5' long. Cut other strips the width of the cover, less 2", and glue into one strip of about the same length.

35. Remove cardboard and, using a damp sponge, rub both sides of the edges of the cover lightly to soften the glue.

36. Dampen the narrow strip and wrap lengthwise around the cover and hold in place with glue or gummed tape.

37. Dampen the wide strip and wrap it around the book in the other direction and fasten it. If the strips are properly centered, a corner will be formed. Care must be taken to shape the corners with the fingers before putting the book away to dry. Allow 24 to 48 hours for the covers to dry, and then strip off the binding paper.

Chapter 15

Repairing Books

Thus far little has been said about repairing books. The point must be made at this time that it often proves expensive to repair a book, when it needs to be completely rebound. *Repair should be temporary and for emergency purposes only,* and the book should receive the attention of an expert binder as soon as possible.

Too often books with broken backs and loose covers receive the "adhesive tape" treatment and are returned to service when rebinding would have been more satisfactory and more economical. For example, when a book has been torn from its cover, the owner must choose between a "make-do" repair or rebinding. In this instance, the best method is also the cheapest, for it would be most economical and certainly more satisfactory to apply new endsheets and rebind the book in its cover. One of the most common, though unsatisfactory, methods of repairing such a book is by gluing or pasting the back of the cover to the back edge (the sewed edge) of the book. The experienced binder knows that this makes the back of the book extremely stiff and that it will soon break down. Adhesive tape is sometimes used by an untrained person to hold the cover to the book. This places all the strain on the outer edge of the book, and again it is a potential source of trouble. Another "inexpensive" solution to this problem is the use of a double-stitched binder. Without belittling a commercial book repair, the expenditure

167

of the same amount of money would have repaired the book in a completely satisfactory manner.

The following paragraphs show methods of treatment of specific repair problems.

Repairing Torn Pages

Slightly torn pages, or pages which are torn well into the reading material, should be repaired by applying transparent gummed tape on one side over the entire length of the torn place. Badly torn pages should be repaired by applying a piece of this same kind of tape to both sides of the page. Clear tapes which will not change color are available. As was stated earlier, this method may be used on textbooks or other "expendible" volumes. On regular library books and other books af considerable value, a fibrous Japanese tissue paper and paste should be used. *Never* attempt to repair a valuable volume until you have developed a basis for judgment. If you are ever in doubt, seek the advice of an expert.

Repairing a Book With a Few Loose Pages

Sometimes pages in a book have been torn out and the margin next to the sewing is gone. This margin should be "built up" by using a good bond paper and gluing a strip wider than the original margin to the inside of the page. This should then be cut to the size of the original page and tipped back in place.

When one page is torn out at the fold of the section, the corresponding page in that section will also be loose. If these pages separate at the fold, each can easily be tipped back into place. Where the torn edge is ragged or uneven, a new margin may be built up with a strip of paper and transparent tape.

Sometimes it is good procedure to glue or tip several loose sheets back into the book, provided the workman does not glue the edge more than ⅛". Loose pages or plates ordinarily should not be glued more than this amount. *Generally, when a number of pages start to loosen, it is wise to resew the book and put it back into its original cover or rebind it in a new cover.*

Repairing a Book With Many Loose Pages

Books having many loose pages should be torn down, re-sewed, and rebound, because it is poor procedure to tip each page back into the book. The glue or paste makes the joint stiff and causes a new fold in the page, which soon tears out.

Repairing a Cover Broken Loose at the Joint

Books with broken joints are quite common, because all that held the book to the cover at the joint was a thin endsheet and a piece of super cloth of insufficient strength. The back edge of the book was not fastened to the cover in any manner, and this caused further strain at the joint.

Double-stitched binders may be used for this repair as a temporary measure where the book must continue in service for a time.

The easiest and most satisfactory method to make this repair is to cut two endsheets the length of the book and twice its width. Fold these in the middle, making the sheets the exact size of the book. After the book has been removed from the cover, glue the two endsheets about $\frac{1}{4}''$ along the folded edge on one side of each and place them in position on the book so that the folded edge is flush with the back edge of the book— the glued side toward the book. Cut a piece of super cloth, muslin, or backing flannel—$\frac{1}{2}''$ shorter than the book, and the width of the back edge of the book plus 4". Backing flannel is recommended because of its strength. Glue the back edge of the book and apply the backing flannel, allowing it to extend over on each endsheet about 2". Round and back the book. Apply a spring back, and "hang-in" the book. Glue up the endsheets and press the book (Processes 25 and 16). This method eliminates the use of a joint strip and can be used where the book does not require new sewing.

In recasing the book in its original cover, sometimes it is necessary to "cut-out" about $\frac{1}{8}''$ from both covers along the joints so the cover will admit the added "swell."

Repairing a Badly Worn Cover

It is recommended that a book with worn covers, but good sewing, be put into a new cover. The best method would be to apply new endsheets and follow the procedure as outlined in Processes 19 to 26.

Sometimes a book with worn covers is in good shape except that the back lettered edge has been torn off. In this case, cut a piece of coated fabric or book cloth 1½″ longer than the cover, by 3″ plus the width of the back edge of the book. Cut a lettering strip of endsheet paper, ragboard, or redboard—the length of the cover and the width of the back edge of the book. Glue the lettering strip in the center of this piece of material on the unfinished side, Figure 110. If the workman uses a machine for lettering, the title and author should be lettered at this time.

If the lettering is to be by hand or electric pen, use tipping strips to cover the lettering strip and glue the entire portion of the material around the lettering strip. Use a pair of shears to cut down from the top and bottom edges of the binding material to within ¼″ of the corner of the lettering strip, as shown by dotted lines in Figure 110. Fold flaps A and B over

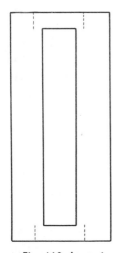

Fig. 110. Layout
of Back Repair Strip

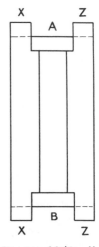

Fig. 111. Making Up
Back Repair Strip

onto the lettering strip (Figure 111) and place lettering strip and binding material over the back edge of the book and rub the binding material onto the old covers allowing flaps x and z (Figure 111) to extend out from the covers. Open up one cover and fold in the flaps marked x; then open the other cover and fold in the flaps marked z. The book may now be lettered by hand.

Repairing a Broken Back

You have seen the book with a broken back—a book which always opens at one place. This is caused by the reinforcing material breaking down along a section. Using the book as a brief case for carrying pencils, papers, and the like causes this failure. Broken backs may sometimes be avoided by breaking down the book when it is new by opening the book a few pages at a time until all of the pages have been opened up flat.

If the sewing still has life, follow the procedure as outlined in "Repairing a Cover Broken Loose at the Joint," being sure to remove most of the old reinforcing material.

Repairing a Book With Loose Sections

Follow the procedure outlined for "Repairing a Book Which Has Many Loose Pages."

Fig. 112. Titles from Old Covers Glued to New Covers

Repairing Old and Valuable Books

Before you do any work on old books, experienced book collectors should be consulted as to what to do. Many times just the putting on of new endsheets cuts down the monetary value of the book. After advice has been obtained, the best procedure should be followed in terms of what the book needs.

Lettering Repaired Books

On books which have been rebound or the covers repaired, the lettering on the back of the old cover may be glued over the new back strip. The title on the front of the cover may be stripped from the old cover, trimmed, and glued to the new cover as in Figure 112. If the workman has trouble in getting these labels to stick to coated fabric, use an adhesive coating (formula in Chapter 4) by applying a coat of it with a piece of cotton over the surface to be glued. Let coating dry before applying labels.

Chapter 16

Bookcraft Projects

The amateur craftsman may wish to vary his binding work and in order that he may see the many possibilities his equipment offers, several special projects are described. There is no limit to the variations possible, and he will readily see dozens of other problems from which he will derive much enjoyment.

A Single-Section Book

A simple problem which has much use as a "phone-number" book, address book, diary, or recipe book is easily made. After reading these directions, the craftsman may vary his materials or methods to suit his own taste.

Procedure

1. Secure about 25 sheets of $8\frac{1}{2}''$ x 11" typing paper.
2. Fold, making a $5\frac{1}{2}''$ x $8\frac{1}{2}''$ section.
3. Cut and apply endsheets and joint strip as described in Process 6.
4. Punch book according to Process 9.
5. Sew book using saddle stitch method, Process 12.
6. Apply reinforcement material—backing flannel is best. Cut a piece of this material $\frac{1}{2}''$ shorter than the book and $\frac{3}{4}''$ wide. Glue $\frac{1}{4}''$ on either side of the sewing on the back of the book and put the flannel on this glued strip.

173

7. Trim the book, Process 15.

8. Cut the covers from **E** binders board (Figure 46). Cut ⅛″ narrower than the book is wide with the "square" about ⅛″ at the top and bottom edges (definition of square in Process 19). Mark one cover **F** and the other **B** to distinguish between the front and back.

9. Select binding material and follow instructions in Process 20 for cutting.

10. Make up cover, omitting lettering strip because this small book cannot be lettered down the back (Process 21). Cut corners if you are going to turn a nicked corner, otherwise use Process 22.

11. Glue edges of binding material and turn top and bottom edges and corners (Process 22).

12. Letter or paste a label on the front cover.

13. Hang in (Process 24). In this step only the space between the covers is glued. Rub joints well with the bone folder.

14. Glue endsheets.

15. Press. Tins may be omitted and lightweight cardboard substituted.

Loose-Leaf Binder

This problem may be used as a scrapbook, notebook, photograph album, autograph book, or the like. It can be any size or any suitable shape.

Procedure

1. Select sheets or pages to be used in the book.

2. Cut two pieces of **C** or **D** binders board, Figure 46. If the page is a large one, use **C**; if it is rather small, **D** is better. Cut this material ½″ longer and the same width as the sheet. Width here is the distance from the back to the front edge of the cover.

3. Cut a ¾″ strip from each cover board on the edge which is to be the back edge of the book.

4. Lay the ¾″ strip and the cover from which it was just cut in its original position and then separate them ¼″. This is done to measure for binding material.

5. Cut two pieces of binding material, allowing a 1″ turn-in on the top, bottom, and front edges and 2″ beyond the ¾″ strip.

6. Glue one side of each of the two cover boards and place on the pieces of binding material so that a 1″ margin is formed on three sides.

7. Glue the ¾″ strips on one side and place them on the binding material ¼″ from the larger boards on the side where the most turn-in exists. Be careful to have tops and bottoms in line.

8. Cut the corners as shown in Figure 113.

9. Glue the binding material all around the boards and, using the bone folder, turn in top and bottom edges.

10. Turn in other two edges, forming a nicked corner (Process 22), being careful to turn the 2″ strip back over the ¾″ board, the ¼″ space, and onto the larger board.

11. Use the straight edge of the bone folder to press the cover material into the ¼″ space, forming the joint.

12. Cut two pieces of endsheet paper, each ¼″ shorter and ¼″ narrower than the large board in the cover.

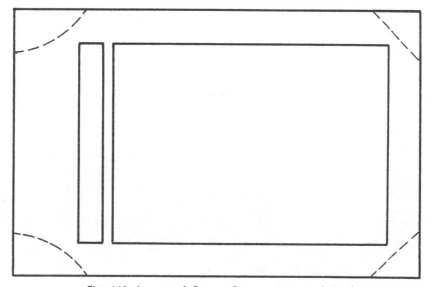

Fig. 113. Layout of Corner Cuts on Autograph Book

13. Glue one side of each of these endsheets and place over the large boards in covers, allowing ⅛″ margin around three edges. Do not allow this endsheet to come over into the joint—it will not do so if it is properly cut.

14. Place covers between two scrap pieces of binders board, weight with wrapped bricks, and allow to dry.

15. Letter or glue label on front cover if necessary. A panel effect can be made by cutting a piece of 22-gauge galvanized iron of suitable size and pressing it into the cover before the endsheets are put on in Step 13.

Fig. 114. Completed Autograph Book Covers

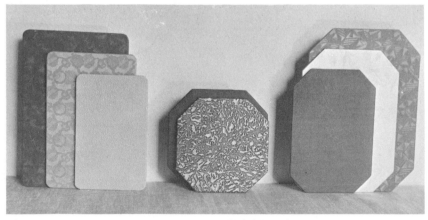

Fig. 115. Hot-Dish Mats

16. Punch two or three $\frac{3}{16}''$ or $\frac{1}{4}''$ holes in the page material, depending upon the width of the binding edge.

17. Place one page on the covers, in its exact position, and mark the location of the holes on the $\frac{3}{4}''$ strip.

18. Punch holes in the $\frac{3}{4}''$ strip.

19. Place the pages in position between the covers and fasten them with thongs, cord, braided lacing, binding posts, or in any other suitable manner. Figure 114 shows two finished autograph books.

Hot-Dish Mats

Attractive hot-dish mats of all shapes and colors may be made from small scraps of binders board, pasted chip, compo board, celotex, or asbestos board. Many sizes and shapes, such as are shown in Figure 115, may be made. After the size and shape of the hot pad have been decided upon, make the pads as outlined in the following procedure.

Procedure

1. Prepare a pattern from heavy paper the desired size of the dish mat.

2. With this pattern, lay out as many dish mats as desired in the boards to be used and cut them.

3. Cut the material which is going to be used to cover the boards about $1''$ larger than the pattern on all sides (coated fabric is a good material for this purpose, as it is heat resisting, waterproof, and easily cleaned).

4. Glue the board on one side and place it in the middle of the coated fabric or whatever material is being used.

5. Cut the corners for the turn-in as in Process 22.

6. Glue the coated fabric or vinyl which extends out beyond the edge of the boards.

7. Turn the edges and corners, using Process 22.

8. Cut a piece of coated fabric $\frac{1}{8}''$ smaller than the board all the way around. This is used to line the bottom side and may be of contrasting color if desired.

9. Glue this piece and place in position, leaving an equal margin all the way around.

10. Place under boards or weights to dry.

Hard-Cover Notebooks

This type of notebook is for all-around use and should be used where strength is important. Figure 117 shows a group of finished hard-cover notebooks.

Procedure

1. Select the size of the paper that is to be used. Find the size of the covers according to Figure 116 column 3, for the size of paper selected if you use a $\frac{3}{4}''$ ring size fixture. Add $\frac{1}{4}''$ to the width if $1''$ ring fixtures are used.

2. Cut two pieces of binders board the size determined above.

3. Cut a piece of binders board at least $1''$ wide, depending on the width of the fixture. It should be the same length as the two covers previously cut.

4. Place the two covers on the workbench with the $1''$ strip centered between them, allowing $\frac{1}{4}''$ on each side of the strip.

5. Cut a piece of binders material so that there will be a $1''$ margin all around the covers when laid out in the above position. Scraps of coated fabric, buckram, or vinyl may be used if the workman wants to make a half binding out of the notebook. In this case, the corners should be cut according to the composite method in Process 28, and the width of the back should be $4''$, plus the width of the back strip of binders board.

Size of Paper	Number of Holes	Cut Covers
1	2	3
5 x 7¾	3	5¾ x 8¼
5½ x 8½	3	6¼ x 9
6 x 9½	3	6⅞ x 10
8½ x 11	3	9½ x 11¾
8 x 10½	2	8⅞ x 11

Fig. 116. Sizes of Covers for Notebooks — ¾ " Ring-Size Fixture

6. Glue the covers in position on the coated fabric as laid out in Step 4 above.

7. Turn the edges of the binding material, Process 22.

8. Cut a piece of binding material of the same color as used on the outside of the notebook, ¼″ shorter than the length of the cover, and 4″ wide.

9. Glue this piece down the center on the inside of the notebook over the back strip and the joints. Rub the material into the joints.

10. Cut two pieces of endsheet paper or some kind of lining material, ¼″ shorter than the length of the cover and ¼″ narower than the cover.

11. Glue these on the inside of each cover so that there is a ⅛″ margin all around.

12. Allow the cover to dry between boards at least twelve hours.

13. Place the notebook fixture in position, centered on the back strip, and mark where the holes are to be punched for the rivets.

14. Punch the holes, using a hand punch or a leather punch and a mallet.

15. Rivet the fixture into the notebook. Use a center punch and hammer to spread the rivets, or use "jiffy" rivets which are hammered together.

Fig. 117. Completed Notebook Covers

Score Pad Covers

The measurements for the covers should be taken from the score pads. Care must be taken in buying the pads so that they are standard size. If this is uncertain, a good supply should be purchased so that extra fillers will be on hand. Use the following procedure in making the covers.

Procedure

1. Cut two cover boards $\frac{1}{2}''$ wider than the score pad and $\frac{1}{4}''$ longer. Use **D** binders board (Figure 46) or equivalent for this purpose.

2. Cut one piece of redboard or lightweight cardboard the same width but $\frac{3}{8}''$ shorter than the cover boards.

3. Cut a piece of binding material so that there is a $\frac{3}{4}''$ margin all the way around the covers when they are laid in position, with a $\frac{1}{2}''$ space between them for the fold.

4. Glue the entire piece of binding material and place the two covers in position, leaving a $\frac{1}{2}''$ space between them.

5. Cut the corners at a 45° angle to the board and about $\frac{1}{4}''$ from the corner of the board.

6. Place the piece of ragboard or cardboard over one of the covers so that it is flush with the edge of the cover on the three edges where the binding material will be turned over.

7. Turn long edges over. Turn a nicked corner, Process 22. A round or library corner may be substituted by following the proper procedure.

8. Cut a piece of lining material, preferably coated fabric of contrasting or harmonious color, $\frac{1}{4}''$ narrower than the covers, and $1''$ longer than the entire length of the two covers plus the joint. Cut this into two pieces so that one will be $\frac{1}{2}''$ longer than the redboard pocket. The workman will readily see how this could have been done with two small pieces.

9. Using a pair of shears, cut the material which covers the edge of the pocket, cutting toward the outside of the cover but stopping within $\frac{1}{8}''$ of the edge. A pocketknife can be used. Begin the cut $\frac{1}{8}''$ from the edge, cutting toward the **center of** the cover as shown in Figure 118.

10. Glue the piece of lining, cut in Step 8 above, and place it over the pocket with a $\frac{1}{8}''$ margin on three sides.

11. Turn the ¾" extension of the lining into the pocket with the bone folder, and rub this material so that it sticks at all places.

12. Cut the other piece of lining so that it overlaps the pocket opening ½".

13. Glue a piece of lightweight coach wadding in the joint, being careful that it does not extend onto the cover material which was turned in (Step 7). Sufficient glue may be applied with the fingertip. This wadding prevents a hard joint from forming.

14. Glue the remaining piece of lining and place it in position on the other cover, and push the end down into the pocket. This may be accomplished by using a bone folder. The edge of the pocket may be kept free of glue by cutting a piece of tipping strip the width of the pocket and folding it around the pocket. After the second piece of lining has been put into the pocket, this piece of paper may be removed.

Fig. 118. Cutting the Pocket on a Score Pad Cover

15. The cover should now be allowed to dry for twelve hours under boards or bricks before putting the score pad in it.

16. Cut off about one-half the length of the back cover of the pad and insert the remaining part into the pocket. The pad is now ready for use, Figure 119.

Research and Study Projects

As you have worked your way through this volume, you have barely started on the "education" to be gained through bookbinding. The bindery itself and the skills which can be developed there are but a small part of the whole field. There is a great area for study in the materials of binding, the historical development of processes, and the gradual evolvement of today's well-designed books.

If *The Binding of Books* is used as a text in secondary school or college classes, a regular part of course work might well include assigned readings to expand the student's concept of the contribution the graphic arts have made to society. Such topics might include:

1. The reduction of gold to gold leaf—here the student becomes aware of the extreme malleability of the metal and its importance and use in industry.

Fig. 119. Completed Score Pad Covers

2. Papermaking—few other commodities come as close to the daily life of man as does paper. From the time an individual opens his daily newspaper through to his use of "folding money" in payment of bills, paper is used. It acts as a can label, it receives print on the pages of a book or magazine, it covers walls, it wraps packages, it carries messages through the mail, it brings joy to the housewife and problems to the merchant as it becomes a trading stamp. Add a thousand other uses of your own. In the bindery it is on every hand, and in the printshop it is one of the basic materials of the work.

3. Inks and ink making.

4. Type design, the history of movable type, and linotype and monotype.

5. The silk screen process and its uses.

6. The Library of Congress.

7. Adhesives—paste, glue, cement.

8. Perfect binding.

9. Photoengraving.

10. The making of coated fabrics and vinyl.

11. The art of illumination.

The topics listed above will provide starting points in the development of appreciation of the multi-faceted craft of bookbinding. Further understanding can come from the use of films and filmstrips. You may have a film rental service close to where you live. Check with them to see what may be available.

Like so many other worthwhile activities, bookbinding involves study and work. But to the interested person, few things can match it for the pleasure and satisfaction it can bring.

Index